Praise for *A Sense of Something Greater*

"A truly surprising, brilliant, and wonderful book. Reading it, you suddenly see that there is something greater that is before us, right here, right now. Les Kaye and co-author Teresa Bouza reveal a different kind of mind (and heart) in the midst of Silicon Valley and of our lives. This marvelous book is not only about the search for balance but for meaning in the midst."

—ROSHI JOAN HALIFAX, Upaya Zen Center, author of *Standing at the Edge*

"Zen meditation may call forth images of Japanese rock gardens and old monasteries, but Les Kaye places it naturally in the midst of twenty-first-century urban American life. Using interviews with individual practitioners by Teresa Bouza, *A Sense of Something Greater* vividly illustrates how this simple practice can offer remarkable clarity and ease to those who work in competitive, high-tech, high-stress settings."

—KAZUAKI TANAHASHI, *Painting Peace at a Time of Global Crisis*

"A warm, remarkably intimate introduction to a spiritual community in the heart of Silicon Valley. Through personal interviews with the community's members, we meet the real people of the Valley, as they struggle to find their bearings in the fast lane of the high tech world; through the wise counsel of the community's leader, Les Kaye, we are welcomed into the ancient tradition of Soto Zen, where meditation is our most natural act and spiritual practice is its own reward."

—CARL BIELEFELDT, Associate Professor of Religious Studies, Stanford University

A Sense of Something Greater

A Sense of Something Greater

Zen and the Search for Balance in Silicon Valley

Les Kaye and Teresa Bouza
Foreword by Natalie Goldberg

 **PARALLAX PRESS**

BERKELEY, CALIFORNIA

Parallax Press
P.O. Box 7355
Berkeley, CA
94707

parallax.org

Parallax Press is the publishing division of
Plum Village Community of Engaged Buddhism, Inc.

Printed in the United States of America by
the worker-owners of Thomson-Shore, Inc.

Cover and text design by Joshua Michels
Cover photo by Jose A. Bernat Bacete/Moment/Getty Images
Les Kaye author photo © Lee Marsullo
Teresa Bouza author photo © Vanessa Able

ISBN: 978-1-946764-21-8

Names: Kaye, Les, author.
Title: A sense of something greater : Zen and the search for balance in
  Silicon Valley/Les Kaye.
Description: Berkeley : Parallax Press, 2018. | Includes bibliographical
  references.
Identifiers: LCCN 2018010892 (print) | LCCN 2018023063 (ebook) | ISBN
  9781946764225 (ebook) | ISBN 9781946764218 (trade paper)
Subjects: LCSH: Religious life--Zen Buddhism. | Spiritual life--Zen Buddhism.
  | Employees--Religious life.
Classification: LCC BQ9286.2 (ebook) | LCC BQ9286.2 .K393 2018 (print) |
DDC
  294.3/92709794--dc23
LC record available at https://lccn.loc.gov/2018010892

1 2 3 4 5 / 22 21 20 19 18

To all dedicated seekers
whose quiet passion for truth inspires lives of authenticity
and the determination to bring forth the highest values.

Contents

Foreword by Natalie Goldberg

After doing deep Zen practice for many years in the heartland of Minnesota, I heard of a book in 1996 called *Zen at Work*. The title alone intrigued me, written by a man named Les Kaye, who worked for IBM in San Jose. *Zen at Work* combined two of my passions—Zen and being employed in the world. Since I was sixteen I have always had a job, and as I've grown older I've realized what a privilege it is to find meaningful work. Work gives us a structure, a way to face our day and to connect daily with other people, not necessarily ones we like or would meet otherwise—it gives us an opportunity to grow and face the challenge of acceptance, tolerance, and cooperation.

Work can also become painful, toxic, and unbearable in an unhealthy environment. Many people say work is by far the biggest cause of stress in their lives. This problem is even more pronounced in Silicon Valley. With the rapid growth of technology companies and startups in the region has come an emphasis on longer hours and frenetic energy. It seems like the human employees are trying to keep up with the machines they are working on and with. This is impossible—human beings are not machines. So many people are drawn to the technology industry—its creative cutting edge, its addictive high energy. But, how to handle your life in the midst of it?

How brilliant that Les Kaye, so many years after his first book and with the encouragement of coauthor Teresa Bouza, has come forth with *A Sense of Something Greater*. This book and what it examines is such a necessary balance, companion, and antidote to the speed and demands of working in the high-tech industry. Kaye's writing is derived from the direct experience of living and working in the Valley for decades. This is not an abstract Zen book about principles of ancient teachings. And his Zen students at Kannon Do Zen Center, with whom he works and who are interviewed here, are not rarified ascetics or hermits but people rooted in the work of the Valley. The book's foundation comes right from the floor of the office building, the factory, the people who live and work there day by day.

Kaye and Bouza alternate commentary and short Zen teachings with interviews with therapists, executives, engineers, and teachers—people who exert effort daily to make alive Zen practice in the workplace. These interviews authenticate the teachings. They are searching and the questions are relevant to each person. They are real conversations, and Bouza carries a respect for what the interviewee has to say. This is Zen in action—how practitioners apply the teachings to bring more intimacy, cooperation, and peace to tech culture.

It is my hope that everyone reads this book, especially in light of our difficult times, but also that more of Zen practice in our country follows in this path, going right to the heart of human action and looking at how the practice can continue to be a tool for freedom, not only in the zendo but right out in the nitty-gritty of commerce where our lives are actually lived.

Natalie Goldberg
November 2017

Preface

I began work as an engineer at IBM in the mid-1950s, in what was then the rural, southern edge of San Jose. IBM had purchased twenty acres of farmland and pasture to develop facilities for the latest in manufacturing, engineering, and research in business computing. It turns out we were at the forefront of a major regional transition. Ten years later, the transformation of Santa Clara Valley from the "Valley of Heart's Delight" to "Silicon Valley" was in full swing. Orchards and farmlands were being replaced by high-tech office buildings and factories, along with the freeways, shopping centers, and homes necessary to support this growing center of creativity, commerce, and the quest for knowledge. This change from a simpler, slow-paced life has now been taking place for decades, not just in Silicon Valley, but also in New York, Seattle, Phoenix, Portland, Charleston, Washington, DC, and Austin, Texas.

It was during this time of transition from farm to factory that I discovered Zen Buddhism. I'd grown up on the west side of midtown Manhattan, found my way to what was to become Silicon Valley, and got a great job with IBM, but the side of life we call *spiritual* was not in the equation. Then on a Friday evening in 1961 at a cocktail party, I spotted *The Way of Zen* by Alan Watts on my hostess's bookshelf.

It caught my attention, and I asked if I could borrow it over the weekend.

At the time, my wife, Mary, and I lived in a two-room cottage on a pear ranch off Skyline Boulevard, near Los Gatos. It was autumn, and the days were chilly and damp. That Saturday morning, I lit a fire, and for the next two days I sat immersed in Alan Watts's magical descriptions of the history and practice of Zen. I was fascinated to discover a dimension of living, an approach to life I hadn't thought about before. When I closed the book, I knew that my technically-oriented workaday life was incomplete. I needed reflection too, a way to connect with and explore my self and the life of spirit. Watts's description felt profoundly authentic, pointing to depth I'd been seeking without even realizing it.

A few years later, I discovered a group of like-minded individuals—businesspeople, parents, stay-at-home moms, engineers, schoolteachers, and grad students—who met regularly for meditation in Los Altos, and I started Zen practice with them. "It's astonishing so few can create such beauty," one of the members commented. Shunryu Suzuki, known by the honorific title *roshi*, meaning "old teacher," had arrived in San Francisco from Japan in the late 1950s, establishing the San Francisco Zen Center and later Tassajara Zen Mountain Center. In the mid-1960s, Suzuki offered to host a weekly meditation group on the peninsula that grew into "Haiku Zendo," a seventeen-seat converted garage in the home of Marian Derby in Los Altos—seventeen corresponding to the number of syllables in a haiku poem, and "zendo" being the Japanese term for "meditation hall." We met one evening and one morning every week for meditation and a short talk by Suzuki-roshi.

At first, the meditation practices and the rituals (chanting, bowing, offering incense) felt strange, but in just a few months, I started to recognize the universal nature of what we were doing.

Although the practices were specific and had cultural resonance, Suzuki-roshi had not journeyed to the United States to bring us something foreign. The essence of Zen practice speaks both to universal truths as well as to the specific challenges, difficulties, and doubts we face today.

Four years before I discovered "Haiku Zendo," I had been involved in circuit design and development of new IBM data processing machines. One morning, my manager handed out large three-ring binders describing a new technology. "We are changing the way we do things," he said. "Transistors are being phased out, printed circuits are the new way. You'll find all you need in this manual."

The fat, heavy, IBM-blue notebook contained hundreds of pages of rules for designing circuits. It was obvious that we would be occupied for weeks or months absorbing these rules, followed by years applying them. I also knew this would not be the last major change in the technology, that we would likely be adapting to a new one sometime in the next five years, and again five years after that.

I could see my work and life becoming absorbed in learning and implementing ever-new technologies developed to make machines more productive, less costly, and more reliable. The vision gave me an uncomfortable feeling, not because the goals were inherently wrong; they had potential to create economic and social value. But at this moment I knew that I was no longer satisfied with exploring individual elements of technology, that I was unwittingly following a script crafted by society, family, and school teachers, as well as my own youthful excitement that had diminished over the years without my awareness.

Over the next several days, I thought about what kind of work I would find engaging and useful. What emerged was the recognition of my fascination with the *relationships* of worldly things, how they fit as well as where they failed to fit. I felt most absorbed arranging component parts of a system to work well together, to resolve impediments to the flow of information, ideas, feelings, and understanding. I wanted to engage in helping the multi-dimensioned world of things—human, technical, and natural—exist together in harmony.

I asked my manager if I could transfer to marketing, explaining that I would like to work with a wider range of people in a more varied environment, solving "real-world" everyday problems, comprised of many parts. He looked at me briefly, stood up, and said, "Wait here." He walked out of his office and headed down a long corridor toward his own boss's office. He returned in twenty minutes and said, "OK, you will start an eighteen-month sales training program next week. Bring the other guys up-to-date on your projects." The following Monday, I started a new career—with a new orientation—as a trainee in the IBM San Jose sales office.

My encounter with the technology manuals was a wake-up call, an encounter with myself. The experience revealed how I had been unaware of what held meaning for me, of my vision of life. It was upsetting to learn that I had been sleepwalking. Years later I learned that everyone is at risk of not knowing who they are at the most fundamental level.

That experience and the question I had over fifty years ago are today occurring with increasing frequency in the tech world. Intelligent and dedicated men and women are feeling burdened, devoting an overwhelming percentage of their time, energies, and minds to technology. They sense that their other dimensions have been unengaged and overlooked. They are turning to spiritual practice to discover who they are, beyond profession, personality, ambition, and pursuit of a successful career.

A Sense of Something Greater is based on the premise that humans are fundamentally spiritual. In every culture and society, from ancient, prehistoric tribes and small communities to worldwide religious institutions today, we create rituals and ceremonies that point to something larger than ourselves and our material lives. Instinctively, we seek to embrace and be embraced by *spirit*, by breath, by dancing, singing, and rites of passage, by nature, and archetypes. We sense unseen dimensions we want to incorporate into our lives.

This book is based on fifty years of Zen practice as an expression of spirituality, as well as its practical application in the everyday world of family and work. In Zen, being fully present with body and mind, in quiet contemplation and in everyday activities, is called *practice*. The book includes teachings, along with interviews with Silicon Valley seekers who are learning to express their spiritual practice in the pressure cooker of twenty-first-century life. These practitioners are trying their best to incorporate spiritual practice in their relationships, work, creativity, childcare, safety, driving, financial stability, preparing for retirement, and every facet of life.

Through focused awareness, patience, and generosity, Zen practice reveals our inherent spiritual wisdom, helping us respond creatively to the uncertainties and complexities of our times. My hope is to demonstrate the relevance of Zen to our lives and illustrate how the spiritual and the ordinary continuously converge.

To see a world in a grain of sand,

And heaven in a wild flower;

Hold infinity in the palm of your hand,

And eternity in an hour.

—WILLIAM BLAKE

Prologue

If you've read even a little about Zen and its Golden Age in preindustrial, agrarian East Asia, you're aware of its colorful stories about unusual people. They were irreverent nonconformists, shaking up the establishment of their time. They had little interest in being part of secular life, instead becoming rebels and radicals because they felt constricted by the mainstream's conformity and unenlightened ways of seeing the world. For much of their lives, they lived apart, on the edges. Today we would call them dropouts.

One of the earliest examples was the iconic Bodhidharma, who is said to have brought Zen from India to China in the fourth century. Legend says that he lived in a cave facing the wall in meditation for nine years, turning his back on the patronage form of Buddhism so prevalent at the time.

Baizhang established rules of ritual and conduct for the first Zen monastery in Tang Dynasty China. He insisted on working with his students in the fields, taking care of the gardens, cleaning the temple grounds, pruning trees. When he was eighty, his monks worried that the labor was becoming too difficult for him. They continually asked him to stop, but he refused. One day, they hid his work tools. That night, without saying a word, Baizhang did not take the food that was offered to him at mealtime. The next day, he again refused to eat. On the third day, the students put his tools back in the usual place. Baizhang resumed working and resumed eating. In his evening lecture that night, he said to them, "A day of no work is a day of no food."

At around the same time, Layman Pang, son of a Chinese bureaucrat, relinquished his comfortable, secure lifestyle out of concern for the corrupting influence of materialism and his devotion to spiritual practice. With the agreement of his wife, daughter, and son, he donated his house to the local temple, placed its contents in a boat, rowed to the middle of a nearby river, and threw everything overboard. After that, he and his daughter wandered the country, visiting teachers and spending time in temples. They supported themselves as peddlers, making straw baskets, sometimes living in caves. When asked by renowned Zen master Shitou what he'd been doing, Pang replied, "My spiritual practice—chopping wood and carrying water."

In the ninth century, the well-known monk Linji traveled the countryside, berating and screaming at priests, insulting high government officials, shocking all with his unconventional behavior. It was Linji who devised the method of hitting his disciples, shaking them, and shouting at them to awaken them to see things clearly.

In fourteenth-century Japan, poet Basho roamed the country, visiting well-known teachers to expand his understanding. He often meditated alone in the mountains, and for a time lived in a tree house to focus on his contemplative practice.

The eccentric and iconoclastic Ikkyu spent his later years in fifteenth-century Japan living with beggars and prostitutes, determined to practice Zen outside the temples, bringing it to commoners. At one point early in his journeys, looking for a place to practice, he found a small temple on Lake Biwa in the mountains above Kyoto. He and the abbot lived there alone. The nights were so cold that icicles formed on their blankets. But Ikkyu was prepared to endure all for the sake of deepening his understanding.

In the seventeenth century, the Japanese monk Bankei fought the corrupt establishment of his day. At one time, intent on gaining enlightenment, he lived in a small room outside a temple. It contained neither windows nor doors, just two holes in the wall at floor level—one for passing food in, the other to go to the bathroom. He simply stayed in the room and practiced meditation. It's said that he sat for so long without moving that his rear end bled. When he came out, he preached what he called the Unborn, the unconditioned, inherent spiritual essence that exists before conceptual thinking, ideas, judgments, ego, and desires.

There were less famous Zen figures who also became hermits, eating acorns and sleeping under leaves. Why did they choose to live this way? Why did they give up being part of their societies? Most likely, the choices available—farmer, shopkeeper, peddler, soldier, servant, bureaucrat—seemed too limiting to them. China was continuously in civil war. Corruption was the way of life in the emperor's palace, in the political arena, even in Zen temples. To the famous and the less-famous Zen monks of the time, life in society was not in alignment with the Truth, with the inherent nature of things. For them, spiritual practice was the only way to live authentically.

At the same time, daily life was simpler in the agrarian world of centuries past. People lived in close contact with the natural world, rather than surrounded by tall buildings, freeways, airplanes, and factories. Societies were oriented toward nature rather than toward material progress. To live as a hermit away from worldly distractions was not considered unusual.

Some of the poets and hermit-monks were angry with establishment elites, while others were less radicalized. But all were frustrated by everyday society. They saw the corruption and recognized its cause as greed. They shared a fundamental passion to discover truth and to live accordingly. To find that truth, they instinctively chose to break away from an artificial world and live beyond the boundaries of convention.

Today a quieter, less dramatic waking-up is taking place. People are turning toward spiritual practice because they, like the seekers of old, are motivated to live fully, unbound by the pressures and conditioning of the world. This motivation does not arise solely out of the intellect. We don't wake up one morning and say to ourselves, "Today I'll look for the meaning of life." It is cultivated during quiet, reflective times when we touch something deep within, something difficult to name or describe, a subtle feeling, a sensation, or an aroma, a glimpse of a possibility more encompassing than what usually appears to us in daily life.

What's occurring today in Zen practice is new. It is not the same as in the early days in India or China. It's not about dropping out to pursue practice or avoid worldly distractions. Today's Zen students are part of the general population and have to earn a living to support families: dropping out is not an option. The challenge for today's spiritual seeker is to practice in the midst of difficulties, to be centered and connected with our deepest truth at the very moment that we are confronted by the things that put us at risk of being corrupted. Facing these challenges with determination, going through rather than avoiding the strains and stains encountered along the journey, is the way this path leads us to wisdom and genuine peace.

The vision of Zen practice taking shape in North America and throughout the world today is aimed at discovering authenticity in the heart of daily life, to respond creatively to distractions, not by becoming hermits but by staying in society and finding wise and workable solutions to age-old enigmas. Practice includes helping however we can, in whatever situation we find ourselves, without being concerned about image or attainment. We practice *with* others, not apart. Yet our motivation is the same as in the monks in those far-away times and places. They, and we, understand that career doesn't mean anything if we're not living from truth and that status means nothing at all.

Problems arise when we have only a surface understanding of the truth, when our seeing is clouded by delusion, or filtered and interpreted by other people's opinions that reside in our heads. Zen practice can transform suffering—including the inevitable disappointments and grief—into enthusiasm for life. When we approach the world with a spiritual orientation, everything fits. Everything works together, and whatever we do is helpful. *Zazen* or sitting meditation is not a technique to become someone or something else. We practice to widen our perspective, to see who we are most deeply, what brings us here to this life and this place. *We practice zazen simply to practice zazen*, without a reason. There is nothing to attain.

Each of us is a transient, impermanent expression of something much greater than our everyday self. We live on the earth, yet our movements inherently reflect the Universal, the Absolute, the Holy. When we appreciate this point, we reside in the true spirit of "living in the world." The purpose of Zen is to live without being *attached* to particular ideas or outcomes, or the innumerable material and emotional investments of everyday life. As our understanding grows, we naturally express our universal nature through our ordinary lives.

It can be helpful for some people to live as hermits or eccentrics, but there's no need to do so. Finding our way in the midst of ordinary life is a profound practice. Even if we don't live on the margins like the monk-hermits of old, we can express the same passion for under-standing that they had. We each need to find our own way; for some it's ordinary, for others it's radical. We're guided by what we feel and see of the true nature of things and engage completely in each thing we do. The stories of the elders tell us that it takes effort, passion, and commitment to develop the quality of nonattachment, "seeing"—as Suzuki-roshi said so eloquently and ungrammatically—"things as it is" and actualizing our seeing throughout our lives.

Being is not what it seems,
nor non-being. The world's
existence is not
in the world.

—RUMI

The Price of Progress

Pitirim Sorokin barely escaped execution by the Bolsheviks. After being arrested for anticommunism and condemned to death, he was freed by Lenin and allowed to return to St. Petersburg University, based in part on his highly regarded academic work in criminology and sociology. Four years later, in 1922, he got into political trouble again and this time was banished, eventually migrating to the United States. In 1930, Sorokin was invited by the president of Harvard University to be the first professor and then chair of its new sociology department.

From 1937 to 1941, he published his monumental four-volume *Social and Cultural Dynamics: A Study of Change in Major Systems of Art, Truth, Ethics, Law, and Social Relationships*. Through pictures, tables, charts, and graphs, Sorokin vividly illustrated the cyclical nature of civilization's worldview over a period of three millennia. From the data, Sorokin postulated two major trends throughout recorded history: the *ideational*, where people envision reality as spiritual by nature, and the *sensate*, where materialism prevails. Sorokin interpreted contemporary Western civilization as sensate, dedicated to technological progress, and he prophesied our fall into decadence and the emergence of a new ideational or idealistic era. His visionary work forecast the turmoil of today's world.

Sorokin's model of cyclical change offers evidence that the growing interest in spirituality of the past hundred years, including the growth of Buddhism and Zen in the West, isn't just a fad, but that society has reached a tipping point recognizable by the loss of transcendence and absence of a sense of inclusion in a larger whole. Our sensate society, emphasizing objectivity, ambition, power, admiration, entertainment, and other characteristics of individualism, has overdeveloped to the point of losing its soul and its caring, compassion, humility, generosity, and patience.

We haven't been mindful of the downside of affluence, how it can spoil us and make us lose sight of what we cherish and what enables us to feel nurtured. We've allowed our striving for wealth, pleasure, and excitement to distort our values. When we don't attain the lifestyle we seek, or gain it but then lose it, we run the risk of becoming angry and resentful, a painful demonstration of the Buddha's teaching of desire as the cause of human suffering.

Success and Spirituality

Despite success in their chosen fields and bright prospects for their families, many people in tech, medical, legal, business, and academic professions feel anxious when they reflect on what's happening in their lives. Comments I hear in coffee shops and quiet conversations include: *I need to find some balance. There's no break in my schedule. I feel overwhelmed. I feel saturated with technology. I don't know what success means anymore.*

A few months ago, I conducted a workshop on the relevance of Zen practice for twenty professional women, ranging in age from their early twenties to their early eighties. They were well educated, intelligent, hardworking, confident, well organized, socially skilled, and had lively senses of humor. I asked them to consider these questions: Reflecting on your good fortune in life, why are you attending this workshop? What's going on with you these days?

Their responses were posted on easel paper and discussed as a group:

- Need to find inner peace and reduce the anxiety and panic that has become commonplace.
- I'm trying to do demanding personal skills to maintain sanity.
- Prepare for next phase of life.
- One child launched into career, next is graduating soon, husband looking toward retirement in a few years.
- Family issues.

- Juggling house repairs.
- Learn ways to destress and rejuvenate.
- Organize calmly.
- Feeling distracted with so many different goals, tasks, and things to get done.
- Not feeling settled.
- Can't turn my mind off unless I am sleeping; I can't sit still.
- Deeper self-understanding.
- Desire to fully appreciate my life and those in my life.
- I am here—in this room and in this place in my life—to learn.
- More practice on how to be present.
- To be in community and enjoy people's company.
- To have quiet time, to look at what's next.
- Interested in Zen, inner calm, and peace.
- I experience feeling more alive and engaged with others as a result of meditation practice and wish to enrich that practice even more.
- Onslaught of electronic stimulation.
- Anxiety among those I love.
- Health issues linked to stress.
- Believe in mindful living and deep meditation.
- To be in charge of this hectic life.
- Learn to incorporate mindfulness to lessen worry and stress.
- I'm a marriage and family therapist. I work with preteens and teenagers and would like some ideas how to help them be mindful in their everyday, chaotic lives. I myself have been practicing meditation since I was ten years old, but I get in the trap of the rat race and forget to be mindful.

- To focus 100 percent on task at hand.
- Better sleep.
- Instead of life going by in a blur, how can we better savor the moments of each day?

This list expresses a range of feelings—being overwhelmed, isolated, and out of balance, seeking peace and wanting to fully appreciate life. These women were beginning to think about the spiritual dimension of life and to explore the question of Zen practice and how it relates to work and family. Their comments illustrate that success and good fortune do not, in themselves, address questions of meaning. In fact, we all experience these existential questions and long to be free and live authentically.

In the midst of the demands and pressures of modern life, how do we find the conviction to reflect on these issues? For many, a walk in nature, Sundays in church, or practicing yoga are times when these issues can be addressed. For some, the best medicine is to sit still and be quiet, to meditate on a consistent basis. The motivation to find a place to express and explore questions of meaning emerges out of an intuitive trust and a dim but growing understanding that we are spiritual beings, that there is something greater, that our individual and transient life is a facet of something infinitely large, and we want to touch it, to be intimate with it. We are carried to spiritual practice not just by confusion and concern for creating order in our daily lives, but also by a profound sense of our true nature and of what life can be.

Out of doubt and discomfort, we seek balance, so the pace of modernity doesn't rob us of our humanity. Riding our galloping horse, not knowing how to get off, unaware of the landscape as it whizzes by, the first question is: *How can I slow down?*

I Just Have to Do My Part
Interview with Andy Narayanan

Andy Narayanan completed his chemical engineering degree at the Indian Institute of Technology in Chennai, India, and his MBA at the University of Chicago in 2005. He worked in leadership positions at large and small companies. After more than a decade he sensed that something was missing. He started meditating on his own in 2010 and began formal Zen practice in 2014. Now in his early forties, he is currently working on a new venture in artificial intelligence while being an advisor to other startups.
He is married with two children.

Teresa Bouza: What kind of work do you do?
I work as a product executive in a technology company. I'm an entrepreneur at heart who likes building technology products and companies. I enjoy conceptualizing an idea to solve a real-world problem, bringing people in to a team to transform the idea into a real product that is useful, and then helping the world understand the usefulness of this product. Impacting people's lives by creating products that they can benefit from is fulfilling. For me, this is the essence of entrepreneurship and work.

How did you start Zen practice?
It started with my concerns about work, the work environment we have in this country. I think we need a different approach to how we think about work, and how people work together. Like most people, the way I approached work was influenced by what

I was taught in schools and in work environments, which is to ·
work through a very logical decision-making process. You go
to business school, and learn the different things about how to
run a business. Then as the leader of a company, you demonstrate strength; you lead people by being out in front. That's the
way I was taught. It got to a point where I wasn't happy about
what I was doing. I was working and had a good career. I was in
leadership positions in AI companies, but it didn't feel right for
me. Something was missing. I needed to step back. I did a lot of
soul-searching in terms of "Why am I doing this?" "Why am I
working so hard?" "Why do I want to build companies?" "What is
this thing?" I realized that work is important, and I'd created my
own companies, but I was questioning why I was doing it.

When did this happen?
About five years ago, after twelve or thirteen years of professional
experience. I did everything people suggest that you should do. I
went to good schools, the top business school. I got good working
experience. I followed that path.

What would you say you were looking for?
I was looking for a meaning. It was then that I turned to meditation. I read many books and tried different approaches, and I
finally decided to show up at Kannon Do. I had an "Introduction
to Zen" session and started sitting. After attending some retreats,
I had my first formal meeting with the teacher, Les. After a period
of meditation, I asked him, "Can we chat?"

I found myself saying to him, " I don't know why I am doing
the work I'm doing. What's the meaning of work? What's the
value of zazen? I want to meditate, but I don't know why." He
didn't give the answers I'd hoped for. He just said, "These are

very deep questions. Let's continue to talk and sit together and see what happens."

Each time we met, I asked very logical questions, just as I've always done. "How do I know meditation is working? When am I going to see progress? How long is it going to take? If by a certain time it doesn't work, does that mean I'm not fit for this?" And he said, "I don't know." But there was something about the way he said it or maybe there was a calmness in what we were doing. There was something about it. I didn't know why I was coming back, but I wanted to come back. There was really no reason why I had to come back the second time, the third time, the fourth time, the tenth time. I just decided to show up.

That was two years ago when I first came to Kannon Do, but my search had been on for five years. I had been thinking about this issue in the way you build companies. You are the leader, and it's all about you as a person. You have to be the visionary; you have to be strong; you have to protect the rest of the company from any bad news. You carry a heavy burden; we're taught that you become a leader by being the Superman.

And slowly I realized that's not who I am. The more my journey started unwinding after I started practice, I realized that I was human. I have emotions. Some days are hard, and some days I'm very happy about what's happening. What the practice helped me do was slowly stop reacting to those things and just start observing them. I saw it was less about the individual and more about observing what's happening. When I started doing that, I noticed some changes in how I react to situations.

What kinds of changes?

My approach to leadership was changing. I had a moment when it was like, "It's not about you. Things just pass through you.

You're just one among everything, whether it's emotion, work, output, anything. You're there to do what you are supposed to do." That's how I felt, and it felt great. The pressure began to fall off. I didn't have personal responsibility for everything—building the big business, launching the next product that's going to make millions of people happy. I didn't have to be the one person who makes money and makes everybody happy with their paychecks and bonuses. It didn't have to be only me. I'm just one of the many variables that's making it happen, and I just have to do my part.

That was a very different moment for me, and subsequently I realized that it's less about the traditional leadership style and all the things I'd thought about. It's not about being this fearless leader or knowing everything. It's about understanding the power of everything around you and doing your part, seeing how you can channel and help others. That's the role of a leader.

Monastic Practice in Everyday Life

American culture has been transformed during the past hundred years by the rapid growth of technology and the increasing abundance of material goods. We've witnessed phenomenal advances in communication, health, safety, and comfort, at the cost of possession-obsession and a need for entertainment 24/7. Smartphones allow us to send and receive emails and news at any time, while we ignore those people right in front of us.

When a culture becomes consumed by materialism, its spirit diminishes. Fulfilling material desires isn't enough to provide meaning. It's always accompanied by an empty feeling. When we're more concerned with what we have than who we are, we lose the ability to distinguish between what looks good and what is beneficial. Deceived by appearances, we become slaves to fashion and opinions. Owning fashionable things might be reassuring, but while we're in pursuit of them, we need to be careful not to shortchange reflection, humility, and intimacy.

"What's the point of my life? How do I want to live?" Spiritual *practice* begins when we recognize the ephemeral nature of pleasure and the ways attachment to a particular outcome can distract us from living fully with what is. In spiritual practice, we seek what's *real*, beyond ideas of right and wrong. We want to get to the heart of the matter.

People's ideas about spiritual practice vary greatly. Some are skeptical of the whole realm, concerned it might diminish creativity and drive, interfere with normal life, or be too austere. These concerns are baseless. Material and physical comforts are not inherently bad. Having fun and feeling satisfaction can be terrific. Working and connecting with others can be a joy. It's just that problems arise when we're overwhelmed by or addicted to pleasures, possessions, and the unrestricted ability to do whatever we like, at any time, regardless of others' needs. Consumerism stimulates our desires and attachments and interferes with our clarity, relationships, and peace of mind.

Monastic training offers little of this kind of comfort or pleasure. Monasteries are often located deep in the mountains, where there can be long spells of wet and cold, with temperatures remaining in the twenties, no TVs or smartphones, little free time, and no variation in the prescribed daily routine. Yet, after a while, the mind learns to let go of hoping for "something else" and accommodates itself to this seemingly Spartan life. Monastic training helps us give up striving and become satisfied, even delighted, with basic necessities. The crunch of a carrot at mealtime becomes music, and a closeness develops with nature and other people.

The monk's life provides a mirror for the mind to see itself, to recognize its attachments, and clarify desires and delusions so they can be accepted, and ultimately, let go. The rigorous schedule teaches us how to work on the grounds and on ourselves at the same time. Practice for a time at a monastery can be a great resource. Yet not everyone can take the time from everyday responsibilities to spend weeks or months in monastic seclusion. So we have to learn to practice—to find the mirror—in ordinary circumstances.

The vital ingredient for practice is not a special place. It is the need for courage to accept what we discover about ourselves. It takes determination to continue to stay with the truth of who we are when events are painful and distractions abound. We can practice anywhere, anytime, including our workplace—with its creative energy and stresses—if we remain serious about understanding the truth of our life, beyond appearances. Most importantly, we must face our tendencies.

In his 1973 book, *Small Is Beautiful*, British economist E. F. Schumacher writes, "[The insights of wisdom] ... enable us to see the hollowness and fundamental unsatisfactoriness of a life devoted primarily to the pursuit of material ends, to the neglect of the spiritual."[1] When people recognize the limitations of material possessions and comforts, they seek balance, and they often turn to spiritual practice to find it. A life confined to affluence and excitement leaves nothing to fall back on when we get lost. Spiritual practice can guide us back onto the path toward life's larger meaning.

Material greatness is not a measure of the quality of a society or an individual. Our true measure is seen in our softer, nonmaterial relationships—how we support, care for, encourage, and acknowledge each other. To practice is to recognize that we are always in the presence of something greater than what we can see, think, hear, or feel. We practice because we know that things just come and go, with no permanence. We want to know their source and their meaning.

Scrubbing Spiritual Viruses

Who hasn't experienced a virus on their computer? Despite advances in virus detection, these troublesome packets of code sneak in and create problems and distress. They're malicious creations, unseen and unheard, intent on corrupting and disrupting. We need to detect and isolate these viruses to prevent harm.

Like a brand new personal computer, the mind is inherently *empty*—unselfish, ready to respond to whatever is needed. But just as with our computers, contaminants can creep in undetected, enabling viruses to corrupt our selfless mind.

Here are some common "viruses" that get in the way of our being fully engaged in the world:

- It's too much trouble.
- It's boring.
- I'm tired.
- It's not my job.
- Someone else will do it.
- It's not important.
- How can I make them like me?
- This is good enough.
- I can get away with it.

How do viruses invade our mind? Where do they come from? As interesting and useful as knowing their source can be, it's not as important as is our continued awareness—our vetting process—that allows us to detect and isolate them when they arise. By preventing them from taking over, the mind remains oriented on the big picture, the whole cosmos.

Computer security software runs in the background; it doesn't interfere with the application or the work in process. The attentive mind is the same; it detects what's going on in the hidden places and can protect us. When we become aware of our tendencies, the emotions and habits that interrupt our presence and undermine our intention, it can be painful to fall short of our ideal of who we are and how we want to be in the world. But with honesty and humility, these "interruptions," our self-generated "viruses," can inspire us to live with authenticity. It's as though we're running mindfulness in the background as our security, using skills honed in meditation to support our life's purpose.

It can be challenging to be mindful in a complex, busy, world of distractions. The motivation starts with a problem—a *corruption*—and a feeling of suffering. We want to put an end to it. This is true when a mechanical or electronic device breaks down, or when we detect an emotional or spiritual virus. A problem with a PC, a broken water pipe, or a car that won't start can disrupt our lives and trigger anxiety. We can hire an expert to take care of the PC, the pipe, or the car, but that's where the analogy ends. Our habits, tendencies, and delusions are not mechanical and can't be "fixed" by someone else. Money, outside techniques, or even interventions by those who love us can't resolve our karmic tendencies.

No software or hardware fix, no algorithm, app, firewall, or anti-virus program can help us know ourselves. During an interview in 1975 in Los Gatos, the Zen priest Kobun Chino was asked, "What techniques do you use to encourage people?" He replied, "We use the best technique—people's own sincerity." Continual awareness, the activation of our selfless mind, is our only intervention. Zazen is the best response to karmic tendencies, to prevent being overwhelmed when they pull us away from ourselves. We rely on our own determination to live the Bodhisattva life, compassionately caring for ourselves and others, trusting our own intuition and experience.

We cannot help ourselves if we ignore our karma, mental habits that sabotage the mind. The point of Zen practice is to lead an authentic life, with honesty, without deceiving ourselves, without trying to protect our ego, a carefully crafted image of how we would like to appear to others. When we first begin practice, it can be difficult to accept ourselves as we are, to acknowledge our problems, limitations, habits, stubbornness, and biases. But through continued practice, we develop the discipline and insight to respond to them in creative ways when they arise.

This attitude is known in Zen as awakening our Buddha nature, our true self. Buddha nature knows what to do, knows how to do the hard work. If we don't understand the meaning of working hard, it is impossible to awaken our Buddha nature. By "working hard," I mean continual, undiminished spiritual activity.

In Zen practice, we try to sit in meditation with the determination of a Buddha. When Shakyamuni Buddha left the comfort and safety of palace life to seek the truth, he spent years trying various yogic practices to gain understanding. Finally, he gave up searching for a single technique that would solve his problem. He just sat down and relied on his own effort. Doing so, he woke up to the truth of himself and of the entire world.[2]

Impostor Syndrome
Interview with Dave Redell

Dave Redell retired in 2016 after fifty years as a software engineer, most recently for Google. He's in his late sixties, married,
with two stepchildren. He began formal Zen practice in 2002.
Dave grew up in a Protestant family; his parents chose churches
where the sermons were the most intellectual. So when he first
discovered Zen in the 1960s, he saw it as an intellectual exercise,
something to read about. In 2002, he attended a class at Stanford
taught by Les Kaye. Each class ended with a brief meditation,
and Dave began to realize that Zen is something to *do*. He felt as
though he'd had a wonderful vehicle in his driveway for more than
a decade, and all he'd done was read the owner's manual. He's
been meditating since then.

**Teresa Bouza: How did your Zen practice impact the way you
saw your work and the way you dealt with situations at work?**
I've loved working on computers ever since I was a kid. As I grew
older, I became ambitious about work and developing a reputation in the field. I completed my doctorate at Berkeley, taught at
MIT, then came back to the Bay Area and worked at Xerox PARC,
a great research lab. It was enjoyable, but very anxiety-producing.
I'd constantly reevaluate myself and how I fit into the hierarchy.
Being around so many smart people was intimidating.

Zen practice helped me face this tendency with compassion
and composure and I began to truly enjoy my work. It's exhaust-
ing to always be thinking about how you look—your work defines

you. Zen helped me bring a more straightforward attitude to work and generate much less nervous energy.

I had an interesting experience early in my career at Google, when not only was I practicing Buddhism, but also my boss had been a resident of San Francisco Zen Center for years. Neither he nor I was advancing through the ranks at Google at the rate we might have if we were more anxious and aggressive, but we both found the work itself deeply fulfilling. I was happy there because of my practice. I worked in the field for fifty years, and the last fifteen were the most pleasant because I was able to relax ego-based anxiety and just enjoy the work.

What were your jobs at Google and other places you worked?
Over the course of my career, I went back and forth between managing and being an individual contributor. At the high point of my management career, at Compaq Research, I was Director of Advanced Development, a second-level manager with forty-five people reporting to me. I didn't find that terribly fulfilling, and when I went to Google I thought about management, but chose to be an individual engineer. I didn't really get into computers to manage people. Being an engineer gave me great job satisfaction.

There seems to be a lot of suffering at tech companies because of this extremely competitive environment.
There's a wonderful phrase, "impostor syndrome." People who are wildly successful, very smart, very aggressive, very energetic, work very hard and do very well, yet they somehow feel like they're faking it and if anyone around them finds out, they're doomed. In mild doses, career anxiety might be a motivator, but in higher doses, it doesn't matter how much you "succeed,"

you're never going to feel successful. You're not even going to feel good about what you're doing.

Was it difficult for you to be less intellectual in your Zen practice, since that was such a basic part of your formative years? Where do you stand now?

The framework of starting from a set of ideas, which then leads to practice, is a Western idea. In Christianity, you believe certain things, which motivate you to act in certain ways. In Zen, we practice first, and any intellectual understanding flows from the practice.

Zen books can be kind of like manure. You buy a bunch and stick them on your shelves. If you don't do anything with them, they'll make your house smell. But if you open them up and spade them into your garden, when a seed lands in the rich soil, maybe something good will happen. Reading, thinking, and talking about Zen helps fertilize the soil so the actual seed of practice has a chance to grow.

Now that you're retired and have more time, will you devote more time to your practice?

That's my intent. When I was working, it was difficult to come to retreats and early morning meditation. I remember standing with other practitioners after one of Kannon Do's annual meetings and thinking I was getting a lot more out of the community than I was putting into it. I'd like to balance that.

Is there anything else you'd like to share about the practice and the importance of Zen practice in your life?

Les lectured about the importance of *Sangha*. Buddhism emphasizes the three treasures: Buddha, Dharma, and Sangha. I always saw Sangha as subordinate and supportive, that it's good to have other people around because they encourage us. Now I see that Sangha is, in itself, a jewel.

We go through our lives listening and talking to ourselves, with an endless monologue pouring through our heads. Meditation practice can help us quiet that monologue so it doesn't obscure everything else that's there. In the same sense that zazen silences internal chatter, practicing with a Sangha silences the static between us, creating space for a direct encounter.

When a group of people practices together year after year, the group can dispense with idle chatter and go to a deeper level together. I hadn't realized that before. When the group is together and one person says something that triggers a thought or an image or an insight in you, the pieces start to fall into place.

Ten thousand flowers in spring, the moon in autumn,

a cool breeze in summer, snow in winter.

If your mind isn't clouded by unnecessary things,

this is the best season of your life.

—WUMEN HUIKAI

A Sense of Something Greater

The life story of the Buddha describes a determined, difficult personal journey of a young man who had everything one might imagine a young man might need to be happy. Born a prince in a small kingdom in northern India, he possessed both physical and mental gifts, and was skilled in many crafts and sports. He enjoyed safety, comfort, conveniences, and pleasures. But in his late twenties, he sensed a need for something beyond what life had provided him. He felt disillusioned and unfulfilled by his royal lifestyle and his surroundings. In her 2001 book *Buddha*, respected religious historian Karen Armstrong describes the young man's dilemma: "He had a yearning for an existence that was 'wide open' and 'complete and pure' as a polished shell.... A miasma of petty tasks and pointless duties sullied everything."[3]

His strong feeling led him to leave the shelter of the palace to explore the world outside. He saw for the first time the aging, illness, sorrow, and death that are part of everyday life, and was struck by the suffering that ordinary people experience. Despite the efforts of his father, the king, to keep him at home, the young man left the palace to live an austere life, undistracted by "human pettiness and expediency," to find a way to put an end to mankind's suffering. The hermit's lifestyle was not unusual in India in the third century BCE.

He was encouraged by many other men and women who had left home to become forest monks in order to live a spiritual life.

The legend describes his years of ascetic practice with the leading yogic teachers of his day and his eventual recognition that something was still missing, that he couldn't learn the truth from someone else but needed to find it on his own. His determination was mythic. Just before his enlightenment experience, the demon Mara tried to tempt him to give up the search and enjoy earthly and sensual pleasures. He resisted, staying focused on his goal, and he realized the wisdom that erases ignorance and brings equanimity to troubled minds. Thus, he became a Buddha, an awakened one.

We don't know with certainty what was in the heart and mind of this intelligent and thoughtful young man. But it doesn't take much to imagine that he was troubled by questions and doubts similar to those we experience today, and that he sensed it's possible to meet the vicissitudes and the joys of our lives in ways that are more satisfying, more alive, more vital.

There's a crisis in the world today, much as there was in Buddha's time, during the period known as the Axial Age, from the eighth to the third century BCE, described in Karen Armstrong's *The Great Transformation*. It was the time when most of today's world religions came into being, including Confucianism, Taoism, Hinduism, Buddhism, and monotheism. Disruptive changes were taking place in technology and commerce. People were asking basic, existential questions, like "What is the purpose of my life?" and "How shall I live?"

Over the past three centuries of growing materialism, scientism, and technology, similar questions have arisen. "Is this all there is?" There is now an increasing exploration of spirituality, based on a sense that there must be something greater. We want to live authentically, in sync with the truth of things, to go beyond artificial—man-made—limits of society, culture, and beliefs. We're becoming less interested in doing things simply because of custom or even "common sense." Sensitive and imaginative minds want to seek and discover the greatest of truths and live accordingly. They're willing to accept their own personal flaws and even while working on them to develop their character, to be in the world without compromise. In today's terms, they are asking, "What is my real value added?"

Mind without Boundaries

The writings of Zen Master Dogen, the thirteenth-century founder of Soto Zen Buddhism in Japan, are familiar to serious Zen students. The first fascicle in his epic work, the *Shobogenzo*, concludes with the story of a Chinese Zen teacher instructing his student:

> One day when Zen Master Baoche was fanning himself, a monk approached and asked, "The nature of the wind never changes and blows everywhere, so why are you using a fan?"
>
> The master replied, "Although you know that the nature of the wind never changes, you do not know the meaning of blowing everywhere."
>
> The monk then said, "Well, what does it mean?"
>
> Baoche did not speak, but only continued to fan himself.
>
> Finally, the monk understood and bowed deeply.[4]

On a recent Saturday, we held a daylong meditation retreat under ideal conditions at Kannon Do. The warm, bright weather could not have been more accommodating. We kept the doors open, allowing the gentle sounds of leaves blowing in the courtyard to enter the meditation hall. One could feel the breeze of zazen dispersing all boundaries and distractions. Although the mind creates boundaries to give us a sense of certainty and even importance, they are finite containers imposed on an infinite universe.

Mental boundaries are comfort zones amidst the ambiguity of constant change. But these comforts are artificial; they cannot provide lasting freedom or happiness. We feel compelled to defend these notions, leading to anxiety and doubt. Zazen practice helps us dissolve unwarranted, imposed boundaries and categorizations to find freedom in a world of no boundaries. This is the point Master Baoche was making.

Spirituality pervades the cosmos, just as an aroma awakens recognition of what is nearby but out of sight. Spirituality cannot be measured, photographed, or recorded. It's not exciting, it just *is*. The spiritual dimension is neither objective, rational, nor material; it is beyond form, thought, ambitions, concerns, discriminations, success, or failure. As it has no boundaries, it cannot be grasped or contained, and this can create discomfort. We prefer to stick with what's comfortable or exciting, what we can grasp with our mind. But when the subtle scent persists, when the continuous spiritual breezes enter through open doors, they guide our life and understanding.

After we taste this spiritual dimension, how can we express it, live it, in everyday life? Our stories are important. How did we behave at work or at home or in the line at the supermarket? Stories remind us how to express our spiritual practice, how to maintain good relationships, how to relieve our anxieties, and how to avoid creating problems for others. But beyond the stories, how do we keep in mind that the perceived dichotomy between spiritual and ordinary is a false one? When we separate the two, we lose the wisdom of our spiritual self. The spiritual and the ordinary cannot be separated, but we live as though they are.

Why did Baoche fan himself? Because the answer to the monk's question cannot be found in explanations; how could a verbal response express the nature of wind, or the nature of our essential self? Baoche's silent gesture reminds us that we can be like the flowing breeze, unimpeded by fears, thoughts, or concepts—the activities of mind.

The Source of Compassion

What is Buddhism? What is Zen? As interest in the spiritual dimension of life grows, these questions are being asked more and more. The number of meditation centers is growing, as is attendance at retreats and workshops. Lectures, videos, and blogs about Buddhism can be found on the Internet in abundance.

Many Buddhist texts are now available in English, describing its history, philosophy, and practice. Much has been written, and there's a great deal to learn. But too much dependence on philosophical understanding risks missing the *spirit* of practice. At its core, Buddhism is personal; it expresses itself through living beings, through our feelings, insights, and the understanding we acquire from engagement. Buddhism is based on compassion—an open heart.

Buddhist compassion is not sentimental. It's based on a settled, confident feeling that this messy and chaotic life is inherently *untroubled*, that it's a reflection of something greater than ourselves. When we have the sense that each of us is the expression of this vast reality, our attitude turns toward taking care of our world and all life in it. The mind then is open, and oriented outward.

Buddhist compassion begins with the subtle trust we bring to practice. Without having to know each other's personal lives, inmost secrets, or vulnerable places, we simply, quietly practice together. Through this trust, we develop an intimate friendship with ourselves and with others.

Suffering begins when we haven't learned to be truly friendly to ourselves. It's not that we're mean or indifferent, just that we don't allow ourselves to *be*. We treat ourselves cruelly, pushing to achieve one thing after another to meet overwhelming expectations, particularly in the modern, high-tech work environment. We punish ourselves by not setting aside, for a time, everyday demands and ambitions, to experience life directly without interference from our overly busy mind. When we slow down, reflect, and observe what's going on beneath the surface of our demands, we discover a profound friendliness, a sincere kindness within ourselves. This is why many people come to practice—to remember to be friendly to themselves, with no strings or expectations.

Becoming friends with ourselves—allowing ourselves to be who we are—inherently and naturally extends to friendship toward everything else. Comfortable in our own skin, we can relate to the *whole* world. When we're friendly with ourselves, the homeless person who approaches us is not a threat. When we trust ourselves and develop an intimate friendship with our own being, we won't be desperate to attain lofty goals. What once seemed vital is no longer urgent. With this trust, there's no need to dwell on personal achievement, because we know what we are doing, who we are, and the life we truly want to lead.

A student at San Francisco Zen Center asked Suzuki-roshi, "Why are you a Zen master?" Suzuki didn't reply. The student added, "I'm going to Japan." He meant he wanted to train to become a Zen monk. Suzuki-roshi, understanding the young man's intent, responded,

"Don't." "Why not?" the student asked. Suzuki-roshi explained, "Because you don't know who you are."

When we're not on our own side, we run around trying to find ourselves, reaching for someone else's idea of success. We strive for material or emotional things as treasures to possess, to enhance our image. We don't recognize who we are in a universal or a deeply personal sense. We fill our lives with things and try to influence how people see us.

The things we strive for are not what we need. What we crave most is completeness. We strive to fill an empty space within, believing that possessions will relieve the feeling of emptiness. But the idea of an empty space inside us is an illusion, created by lack of self-knowledge. The best way to satisfy our deep desire for wholeness is through the friendships that come from practice, the practice of intimacy with ourselves and others.

Zen practice has nothing to do with attainment and everything to do with a mind that is generous and open. Practice starts with our self, and without our self-sabotage, our generosity spontaneously extends to others. This is compassion, the fundamental nature of Buddhism.

Admitting You Don't Know
Interview with Colleen King Ney

Colleen King Ney is a psychotherapist. She began her spiritual journey in 1998 after a traumatic divorce that led to alcohol addiction. Now she works with technology companies in Silicon Valley, helping people understand their addictions to doing, achieving, and busyness. She encourages her clients to be more reflective and to get in touch with who they are, what they need, and their own limits.

Colleen started Zen practice one evening in August 2012. After the meditation, chanting, and lecture, she ran to her car and started dancing. The ritual, she says, "triggered something" and encouraged her to continue her practice. Zen practice deepens her relationship to silence. "The gem of it all is that Zen is simple. It helps me connect with the true nature of myself and others. It's deeply nourishing, and I am so grateful."

Teresa Bouza: You've been a therapist for over three decades?
Yes, since 1985.

It seems that therapy as a process is very mental, while Zen meditation stresses learning through your own experience by developing your intuition and being less logical. Have you reflected on this?
As a therapist, I try to help people get on a path where they're more connected to their experience. A shift goes on that opens

them up. It's not just mental or intellectual. It's the experience in the moment.

The analytical part of therapy examines how people move away from their truth, how their past history has created their defenses, and how they defend against their feelings—they don't want to see certain things. You're peeling away layers that obstruct them from their experience. I like to help people look at how they're turning away from parts of themselves they don't want to see.

Zen practice is helpful when one is ready to reflect more, be quiet, and access intuition. To be with oneself is easier after you've peeled away some of the layers. When people say, "I can't meditate," they think they're not ready to do something like that. I usually encourage them to check it out.

I guess slowing down is a challenge here in Silicon Valley.
If you've worked in Silicon Valley for a while, you see the culture of busyness and speediness, that people are discouraged from reflecting; they're just *doing*. I see it all the time in the companies I work with. This busyness affects our thinking, the way we feel, our behavior. A lot of people walk around feeling like failures, trying to adapt to this crazy culture.

Why do they feel like failures?
Everything is about success and doing and being busy, and it's never enough. There's a lack of limits; things are faster and faster, and the technology itself appears to have no limits—the Internet seems limitless; knowledge seems limitless. The experience of just being human and having humility and limits seems passé; it's all so distorted.

There's a lot of delusion about, "I could be better, I could know more, I should do more, everyone else is doing more." They are disconnecting from their intuition and their capacity for reflection; it's about doing and they're getting disconnected from themselves. Even those who are successful don't feel connected to what brings them happiness. That makes them feel like failures.

People ask, "Why aren't I happy? I went to Harvard and I'm here in this big tech company; what's wrong with me?" I don't think they can slow down to check in with themselves, because they're so attached to success and achieving. They don't access what they really want and need and feel.

You're describing a pattern among these highly successful people at tech companies, that they don't feel they are enough. Have you identified other patterns?
Not enough and a lack of acknowledgment that as human beings we have limits. The sense of having limits or humility is out of whack, because there's always more to do. The idea of success is based on money, achievement—more and more and more. It's addictive. As a consequence, they're losing touch with who they really are, what they really need, and just the limits of their bodies. There's always a sense of dread, "OMG, there's another thing I don't know and I could learn it if I sit and watch another YouTube video."

What advice do you give to these people?
Be mindful and pause. Slow down. Yesterday I saw three new people, and they were all out of control.

Meaning what?
Out of control with busyness, time. They don't know their limits. They're not feeling they're enough, there's always more

to do, and there's another promotion they're chasing. Their life is unmanageable in the sense of it's never enough and they're overworking or maybe not even happy with what they're doing. They're not acknowledging that, because they think they *should* be doing this thing they're doing. There's a lack of control; they feel unbalanced.

How do people react to your advice to slow down? Do they think it's possible?
A lot of people ask, "Why aren't I getting promoted and why can't I control my promotion?" They're used to moving ahead and are very dependent on the idea that success is a way of feeling good about themselves. If they're not getting a promotion or they can't control it, they start to feel self-doubt and insecurity, as though they're falling apart.

Are you able to tell if these people are on a path to transformation after you've worked with them?
Absolutely. Some people do get on a path to transformation. How many? I don't know; I see a lot of people. It's about developing a practice in one's life. My work is helping people connect their values and principles with the rest of their life, so they don't feel separated from things vital to their sense of wholeness. That's the priority. In my mind, it has to be a feeling. It's not enough just to analyze.

You really want to see a change, especially in the case of addictions, right?
Pretty much everybody has some kind of addiction. We all have compulsions; we all look outside ourselves for external soothing. The people who are really on this *doing* and *achieving* and *fast pace*

are addicted. There's a lack of self-awareness, of self-growth. It's dependency on things outside of ourselves, such as "If I don't get a promotion, who am I?" They try to do something and control it. It's loss of connection to self, and it can't stop.

How can we overcome addictions?

First, you have to admit you're in trouble. Many people have trouble admitting that what they're doing isn't working. They have denial; they rationalize. People who are attached to busyness also rationalize. They glamorize being busy, as if we're all supposed to be living like that. You admit that your behavior, your thoughts, and your feelings aren't working well, that you have a problem. Then it becomes a matter of how else are you going to live.

I talk to people about having a practice in their life. It's not just therapy once a week or ten sessions, it's about every day. We have to surrender and admit that we don't know everything and that we can't control things. People have trouble with that because they feel like they should be self-sufficient, independent, and a doer, but overcoming addiction is about reflecting, admitting you don't know, admitting you don't have control, and embracing that understanding.

Can you share a little of your own experience with addiction? How did you overcome it and how did your spiritual practice help?

Addiction opened the door for me to spiritual connection. Growth often comes from suffering. The pivotal moment is admitting. I was at a red light on the corner of El Camino and California Avenue in Palo Alto, and I said to myself, "Oh my God, I'm an alcoholic." I admitted I was drinking too much.

I went from humiliation and shame to a journey of humility and transformation. Admitting I can't control something, I realized I needed outside help, something bigger than me to help me. That spiritual nugget opened the door for me to know myself more, to be hungry for transformation, and to get lots of help. I embarked on a journey that has deepened and deepened ever since. For the last few years, spiritual practice has been the priority and the joy of my life. I live and breathe it. My work as a therapist has become much more spiritually focused. I feel very lucky.

Right Effort

Buddhist tradition is more than 2,500 years old, but new to the West. It will take time for us to adapt to a worldview so different from our prevailing paradigms and religious traditions. Buddhism sees the individual as an expression of—but not separate from—something far greater than the person, a viewpoint leading to reverence and humility.

Zen Buddhist practice relieves us of the pressure of trying to win personal advantage. Instead, our vantage point widens to include all things and all of life. It's a spiritual practice based on "anonymous virtue," doing things without trying to get reward or notice.

The closing lines of *Middlemarch*, George Eliot's classic novel of nineteenth-century England, perfectly describe this way of living: "For the growing good of the world is partly dependent on unhistoric acts; and that things are not so ill with you and me as they might have been, is half owing to the number who lived faithfully a hidden life, and rest in unvisited tombs."[5] The attitude of doing inconspicuous, foundational work, without worrying about being admired or even liked, is highly valued in Buddhism. When we live this way, our actions extend far beyond immediate gratification or short-term goals.

Most of what we do today will be forgotten. If we focus on the *intrinsic value* of what we're doing, beyond economic measure, our work is already dedicated to future generations, folks we'll never know, our great-great-grandchildren. Deriving satisfaction from quiet, inconspicuous work, work to which most people do not assign a high value, we experience true composure. When we want attention or notoriety for ourselves, we sacrifice stability and equanimity, and life's universal value eludes us. Acting without ego, our life begins to cohere and have meaning, and we gladly wash dishes, clean toilets, mop the floor, or whatever needs doing—with care and humility.

In Western society, if we're reasonably intelligent, willing to work, and have the good fortune to live in a supportive environment with opportunities for learning, we can do almost anything we like. Others will recognize our abilities and ask us to do something for them. Society offers opportunities with big rewards, material and psychological. But if we use our abilities to do things based on pleasing others, manipulating, or hoarding material possessions, we, in fact, will be used by them and by our own actions. We become puppets, not true to ourselves. We can do something beneficial for others while providing for our families. We need to maintain a stance of doing the small and inconspicuous tasks that come our way, the things society regards as trivial. For our own wellness, we need to resist ignoring or disparaging tasks with little status.

Fame and wealth are not necessary for satisfaction. What's most important is to find our universal self and be who we inherently are. If we strive to be famous or useful to the powerful, we'll lose the meaning of life. If we become proud of ourselves, concerned about our image and how others see us, proud of our reputation, we are relying on the world to grant meaning to our lives. This kind of pride does not nurture. The pride that nourishes us comes from having the deep feeling that we are living a life that nourishes others as well. We have to taste the truth of who we are and what we value directly, through our own effort and awareness.

When we're independent, not relying on anything outside ourselves to define who we are, we will not carry the burden of pride. When we understand the meaning of making an effort for its own sake, we're not consumed about anyone else's approval.

To be independent and confident, we have to be honest with ourselves, see ourselves as we are. It requires sincerity, vulnerability, and openness, not deluding ourselves or denying what we discover. When we become aware that our focus has strayed, we need to come back to our clear, ungrasping mind. Our practice can't be perfect, but when we're aware of our own imperfections and accept them, we will feel quiet satisfaction.

Authentic Life

The meaning of life is not found within the narrow range between birth and death. The truth of our life cannot be analyzed like a classic novel we discuss over coffee. Life is not a story with beginning, end, and moral message.

To truly understand our life, we must view it from the standpoint of the infinite, without limits.

At the same time, its vast meaning is expressed in ordinary, everyday activities, which sometimes does feel like a movie, with a start, finish, and a story to tell. Rather than trying to analyze the meaning of life, we should exercise a broad vision and feel the texture of our experiences in order to know its "whos" and "whys."

We have an absolute life and a relative life—the eternal and the everyday—that exist together without separation. It's important to recognize this dual quality of our nature, otherwise we'll attach to one side without noticing or appreciating the other. We should avoid thinking, "Daily life is more important," or, "Spiritual life is more important." We live in both realms simultaneously, and if we don't notice this, we will be off balance.

In a formal question-and-answer ceremony more than fifty years ago, a student said to Suzuki-roshi, "I have many questions, and I can't choose among them. You are the only faith that is here for me, and I want to thank you." Roshi responded, "Yes, but choose something, and be concentrated on something you have chosen. Choose some problem." She said, "What if it seems insurmountable?" He replied, "Choose something easier." He was advising her to make a decision about everyday life, not to escape it by sticking to the spiritual side of life.

Buddhism has many schools and philosophies, and is rich in its understanding of how life unfolds individually, collectively, and eternally. It provides insight into our dualistic nature and the dualistic way of seeing things, expounded in teachings like the Four Noble Truths, the Eightfold Path, the Twelve Links, the Three Bodies, the Five Aggregates, and so on. These teachings can all help our practice, but most important is how we relate to the world and others in our everyday activities.

We humans are always creating conflict and so continue to extend suffering. It often seems as though this tendency is inherent in human nature. But this suffering can be avoided, and this is the gift of the teachings and the practice. Although it's not possible for us to agree with each other on everything, we can keep our minds flexible so we can understand each other's feelings and ways of seeing the world, leaving space for connection and communication.

During the last election, several homes in my neighborhood had their political signs defaced. This was done by someone frustrated and angry, someone suffering. There was no space in that individual's mind for differences of ideas or dialogue; it was feeling raw and tender, burned, not to be touched. We may feel our own opinion is right, and the other person is wrong. But if we can let go of ideas of right and wrong, we can more fully understand that what we call "right" and what we call "wrong" are two opinions, or views. Even if we're sure we're "right," we can disagree without fighting. If we try to do this by willpower, it will be difficult. But if we can soften our views, helped by our practice of zazen, the practice of "letting go," our mind will have space for the unfamiliar, including opposing views.

Before we appear in this world, something is already here. We can't say precisely what it is; we can't know it in the usual sense. It's not a "thing" that shows itself in familiar ways. Each of us is both form and color, as well as "something" that has no form or color. As we open up and understand our nature that way, it becomes easier to make space for one another, to understand each other without conflict. Then, when we meet someone who feels raw and tender, we just invite her to join us for coffee and give her our attention.

We all want to know our true nature, who we are before we develop a personality and an ego. We want to live authentically, in accord with it. It's not possible to know our true self intellectually; we have to be patient, to allow it to appear and make space for it. Someday, when doing something helpful for another person, spontaneously and naturally, without having given it any thought, you may recognize something about yourself that you had not been aware of or admitted until this moment: "Oh, I can be unselfish!" And you will recognize that there is no need to *try* to be unselfish or to *act* that way because it's a rule. You'll recognize that this is not about pride, or a quality unique to you. To be unselfish is your true nature, as well as everyone's true nature. It manifests naturally, without special effort, from continuous practice.

Choosing Wisely
Interview with Dan Geiger

Dan Geiger is in his fifties. He's been living in Silicon Valley since 1986, when he began his MBA studies at Stanford University. He's now a marketing executive, married with three children.

Teresa Bouza: What motivated you to start practicing Zen?
I had a blow-up at a woman at work. We were working on a joint project. I wasn't getting what I needed from her and I got frustrated. I was stressed and angry, and I yelled at her in public. She was a friend, but she wouldn't talk to me afterwards. I felt really stupid about it. I knew I was doing something wrong. I lost that job five or six months later, and during my time out of work, I started practicing meditation regularly.

My mom died when I was three, and I lived with a number of people who loved me but who were volatile. A lot of my life has been driven by fear—fear of losing something, fear of not attaining something, fear of being found out to be a fake, fear of whatever. It doesn't matter what triggers it; fear creates wars. When we don't know how to work with it, we do unkind things to each other.

Did meditation help you see that?
It took me about five years to get that. After a while, my wife thought I was doing better. I recently took a job that's less stressful. I realized that every time I have more responsibility

than I'm comfortable with, pretty much every time I enter a
new situation, I get stressed, and it isn't good for me or my
family. Now I've taken a job I've done before and know how to do
it, and I'm not anxious. I'm trying to do things throughout my
life that encourage me to be more of who I am, rather than living
in reactivity through fear. Meditation helps me question what
I'm doing, and it stops the busyness and forces me to sit with
whatever is there.

Has the practice helped you be less reactive at work?
I'm being really careful in my communications with people,
way more careful than I was. I've learned the hard way after
sending too many stupid emails and saying things too quickly.
If you take time in how you communicate, you're more likely
to treat other people respectfully. I read my emails twice now
before I send them.

**How is it for you trying to be more careful when everybody
else is shooting from the hip and not thinking twice?**
It's a challenge. Part of it is where you choose to work. It can be
difficult to tell what's on the inside until you're there. I'm lucky,
I'm with a company that has a little older culture and the people
seem to be kinder to each other. In part, that's why I chose to
work there.

**Can you say more about how you're approaching this job
in a different way?**
I want to provide more quality. This includes taking time off to
think about what's important, as well as meditating and doing
therapy. Realizing I've had these repeated patterns, I'm over-
promising less and focusing more on quality. I'm more willing

to say "no," or to offer my opinion without overstating it. In the past, I would talk and talk and talk and be extremely excitable. That's my nature, but I'm trying to be more quiet now and communicate a little more thoughtfully. I think it's a reflection of Zen practice, the awareness I've been working on.

Has your relationship with your family improved as a result of this new attitude?

Yes, I think so. It's not just my new attitude. Two of my kids are in special education situations, mental health–assisted schooling. That has forced me to look at them and be very aware of what they are. It forces me to think more about who I am.

For the past eight years, my sitting meditation has been focused internally, being acutely aware of what I'm going through. I'd like it to extend my practice now beyond myself. I'm trying to feel the other people in the room, to turn the magnifying glass outward. I've learned a lot; now I want to bring it more into the world. How much longer can I just focus on myself? I feel it's time to stop worrying just about myself and embrace the world more.

By being more stable, you're already making a better world and a happier family.

I guess so, thanks. I don't give myself much credit for that. I feel like I have to do more. I'll bear in mind that, in my own way, I'm already doing certain things.

And you're finding success in the corporate world despite the M.O. you've described.

True, I've found ways to stabilize myself and be productive.

There's such an acceleration of technology nowadays that it must difficult to be in the middle of Silicon Valley and say I need to pause.

If you take, like, two years off, you'll miss a technology cycle. It's not like being a dairy farmer, where if you went traveling, you could come back two years later and still know how to tend the cows and make cheese. What people are working on in Silicon Valley will be different and the tools we use will be different. But there comes a point where it's impossible to keep up with all the things that are going on, and you have to let some of it go.

Young people in Silicon Valley see the toll it's taking on their families and parents, and I think they want to live differently. But everybody wants to make money; nobody wants to be less well-off than they are now, so hopefully they'll make compromises.

Do you have any final thoughts about your practice that you'd like to share?

Once you remove everything and get to a very base level, it's a nice place to be. People are generally happy, but then we complicate our lives. The more we can simplify, like through Zen practice, and get to the essentials, the better. I was at a three-day retreat and thought I was in deep meditation. Then I started to see frames, like a film of my life and the things that have happened. I realized that we have choices. We have all these reasons why we can or cannot do something. But at the end of the day, we have to have the courage to love people and be good and be ourselves. This practice can help us see and attain this—realizing we have choices and developing the courage to choose wisely.

Zen is not something to get excited about.
Just continue in your calm, ordinary practice
and your character will be built up.

—SUZUKI-ROSHI

No Longer Exclusive

For many religious traditions, meditation and solitude are foundational spiritual practices. Until recent times, these practices were reserved for "exclusive people"—monks, priests, hermits, and wanderers living in forests, monasteries, caves, or the desert—who dedicated their lives to quiet contemplation. They had neither families nor jobs; no need to commute, meet demanding deadlines, compete in the marketplace, pay mortgages or rent, concern themselves with local politics, find childcare, or master new technologies every few months.

Today, Zen meditation is no longer exclusive. For the past fifty years, it has attracted the general population of the United States and other modern societies. People of all lifestyles, family situations, and occupations increasingly recognize that meditation is not separate or apart from ordinary life—a stand-alone activity—but, when practiced consistently, the basis for a life of equanimity, confidence, and character.

Zen was introduced to the United States toward the end of the nineteenth century. The Rinzai Zen priest Soyen Shaku came from Japan to give a talk at the World Parliament of Religions in Chicago in 1893. The event served to introduce Asian religions to America. In 1951, the well-respected philosopher and Buddhist scholar

D. T. Suzuki—one of Shaku's students—gave a series of seminars at Columbia University. At these seminars, the seeds of the so-called Zen "boom" of the late fifties were sown.[6]

The practice of Zen meditation in the United States gained media attention in the 1950s, with the writings of Suzuki and the notoriety of Alan Watts, Jack Kerouac, Alan Ginsberg, and others of the beat literary scene. In those days, and in the hippie era that followed, Zen was considered an exotic import, an exciting commodity promising revelation of a mystical world and an enlightenment that would free the mind from the difficulties and boredom of ordinary life. Calling oneself a Zen student was a rationale to pursue whatever activities represented freedom and to avoid anything considered conventional or "uptight." Drugs and easy sex were part of the scene, as well as a disdain for responsibilities. At the same time, out of the spotlight, a few dedicated individuals were finding ways to practice Zen and integrate it into their daily lives.

Zen in America has evolved over the past half century. There are now hundreds of Zen centers throughout the country in cities, suburbs, and rural communities. They operate with committed leadership, guidelines for practice, and ethical standards, not unlike traditional Western churches and synagogues. Zen practitioners work in the full spectrum of professions and occupations, from physicians, attorneys, engineers, software developers, and venture capitalists, to teachers, secretaries, waitresses, clerks, carpenters, librarians, and social workers. Many are parents, struggling to balance the responsibilities of family life with those of the workplace.

In the latter half of the twentieth century, schools of Zen Buddhism from Japan, China, Vietnam, and South Korea established themselves in the West.[7] Shunryu Suzuki-roshi, among others, brought the practice and teachings of the Soto school of Zen, founded by

Eihei Dogen, who brought this approach to practice from China to Japan in the thirteenth century. Soto Zen has been more available to the average person, due to its relatively straightforward practice, emphasizing gradual unfolding of wisdom rather than intently seeking for a sudden enlightenment experience.

Something's Missing
Interview with Bonnie Sarmiento

Bonnie Sarmiento works in software and quality engineering at Walmart Grocery. She's in her early thirties, and she began formal Zen practice in 2012. Before that, she attended writing workshops and eventually discovered that sitting helped her go more deeply into her writing. She was also able to see her thoughts more clearly, and by observing her thoughts, obsessions, and fears, became more centered and more intimate with her life and the world in general, feeling less confused as a result. She was working for Hotmail at Microsoft when Google's Gmail took over the market, and considers that time a "good lesson in mindfulness," an example of how no one in leadership can become complacent and think their competition doesn't stand a chance. Bonnie believes it's necessary to have a regular practice for meditation to be truly valuable.

Teresa Bouza: How was life for you before you began to meditate?

I was rushing, always on the go; it was terrible. I'd jump into my car, tie my shoes at the stoplight, and then realize my shirt was inside out and I'd forgotten my phone, so I'd have to go home and get it. It was crazy. I felt so much pressure to do so much all the time, and I realized that if I would take the time to slow down, I'd make fewer mistakes, think more clearly, and be happier.

I also realized that it wasn't enough to go to a retreat a couple of times a year and let the rest of my life be chaotic as I got sucked back into the culture. It was then that I found Kannon Do. I began gradually—at first, once every few months, then every month, then every week, and now I meditate two or three times a week for forty-minute periods. On days I haven't meditated, I sit quietly for at least a couple of minutes before I go to bed. I can drop into meditation now whenever I have five or ten minutes, and it's keeping me sane. It's frantic here. The culture is very high-achieving and go, go, go, pushing people to the max. If you don't stay centered, you're less productive and it's actually not sustainable.

How is your daily practice?

I practice at least a few minutes if that's all the time I have, but I make it a regular practice. The times I need meditation the most, when it will really help me at a critical moment, is when I feel I don't have time for it. I'd think "Let me get my work life in order first. Let me finish this project, then I'll meditate." But before I finished the project I had ten more, so it was a rat race. I was running and not getting anywhere. Finally I said, "Okay, I'll sit for sixty seconds right now," and eventually, "Let me set aside ten minutes." I started really small and was surprised the difference it made to keep that commitment, that promise to myself.

How does your attitude toward work, stress, or emergencies change when you have a regular practice?

Practice helps me see clearly what's actually happening. When emotions arise or there's stress, we think we know what we have to do, but it's often just an impulse. For example, I had a coworker who would tell me to do something different from what my boss had told me. I didn't want to argue, so I went into avoidance mode: 'If I just stay away or keep a low profile, they'll leave me alone.' But it just got worse, and they'd be checking in on me more and more. I couldn't focus on my work. I was distracted.

So I went into the meditation room and just sat with it. I calmed down and let go of everything and realized I needed to talk with my coworker. I needed to explain, "It's frustrating. You're telling me something different from what my boss is saying, and I can't keep everybody happy." I knew it would be awkward, but I finally did it and the person said, "Oh I'm so sorry. I didn't realize this was happening." After that, things got much better. Once I actually talked about it and explained what was happening, there wasn't competitive tension anymore. This isn't my tendency. I usually edge away, but that wasn't working, and I realized that I needed to learn other ways of communicating. By quieting my mind, being quiet and reflecting, I saw what to do.

When did you go from working at Microsoft to a startup?
I began work with the startup in 2012 and was there for two years, until we ran out of money and I had to leave.

How was the experience?
It was what I needed at the time—no office politics, just focusing on solving problems in a collaborative way and doing interesting work. It got me excited about technology again. But then we ran out of funding. What works at one point in life is not necessarily going to work at another point. You find the solution for the moment, but it's not going to save you forever.

The hardest thing when you have a vision like working at a company you admire or being with the love of your life is to keep the balance. Then, when something happens—a management change or you get diagnosed with cancer, life throws you something that changes the whole equation—are you ready to accept that change and not deny it or pretend that nothing has changed? Can you deal with the new circumstance and ask, "How does this change things? How am I going to adapt to this situation?"

Accepting change is very Buddhist, right?

Accepting change is not easy. It means grieving. It means entering the unknown. It means letting go of something. But not accepting change, in the long-term, will hurt much more.

Do you see more people interested in mindfulness practice?

With people burning out and getting sick and the bad press that's coming out about certain companies, there's an increased awareness of a problem, that something's missing from our culture, there must be something else out there. Corporations are opening meditation rooms; that's progress. When I started at Microsoft, I would walk the hallways and wish there was a meditation room right there. And then one day, after maybe three-and-a-half years, suddenly one of the doors had a little sign that said "meditation room." It was an empty room with a carpet. I had wished for that room for years, and suddenly it appeared. I've met some interesting friends through meditation rooms.

Aetna's CEO, Mark T. Bertolini, had a bad skiing accident in 2004. He almost died. Meditation and yoga were keys to his recovery, and he started offering classes to his employees. He also increased the minimum wage and generally tried to create a healthier work environment. Aetna now has much lower costs for employee illnesses and increased productivity. Other companies are following suit.

The culture has been to work harder and harder, and it's making people sick. Some people may need to work that hard, but on average people are overworked. If you give the mind some rest, you actually work more effectively. Awareness is starting to rise, because people are getting sick and burning out.

Q: Anything else that you want to tell me about your Zen practice that I haven't asked?

We have to remember that we're going to die. Remembering that is not a burden, it's a gift, because at the end of our life we're not going to care about what score we got at a performance review. When you die, none of that matters. What will matter are the relationships we had with people. Did we care for people? Did we love people? Were we loved? That's why I work hard now, not to get some award but because I care about the people I work with. I don't want to let them down and I know they'll do the same for me.

Q: Do you think meditation practice has made you more aware of that?

Yes. Practice helps us to see the bigger context of things and not to have so much tunnel vision, like, "I have to have this project done." Everything feels so urgent. Maybe it's important. Maybe it needs to get done, but take a moment to pause and notice a beautiful flower or the sun outside or faces of friends and family members and really be with them, even for a few minutes. It makes a big difference. Take a few minutes to really connect with how big the world is and how we are connected to everything, past and present.

"Attention, Attention"

Once upon a time, in ancient China, the emperor's minister was troubled. In desperation, he went to see a renowned Zen master for advice. He said, "Master, the people are unruly and difficult to govern. Please give me a word of wisdom to help govern them." The master picked up his brush, dipped it in ink, and wrote the calligraphy for "Attention." The minister got angry. "I asked for wisdom and you give me just this! I demand a word of wisdom!" The Master then wrote, "Attention, Attention."

What does this story mean? Why does "attention" provide "wisdom?" How does it help govern the unruly? Many things in life ask for our attention, starting with the basics of living. Spiritual teachings tell us that when we give our full attention, we come to understand the true nature of things in the phenomenal world, the temporary world of shape, form, color, and sound. Giving complete attention enables us to see that everything, without exception, shares fundamentally the same qualities.

Sometimes we humans feel we are the highest form of life and are thus entitled to special privileges over other species. We think this way because of our unique mental and physical skills and capacities. But when we pay careful attention to all of life, we see that all things have the same fundamental nature. A blade of grass is no different from our human self.

When we observe and reflect carefully upon all the people in our lives, we see their sameness as well as their differences. We see how they react, how they create, how they take comfort, how they cooperate, and how they suffer. Through careful attention, we can know how to be in harmony with one another.

When we give attention to ourselves, our mental and emotional activities, the ways we do things, we see how foolish and clumsy we can be. Our character grows stronger when we recognize our mistakes and admit, "I goofed. I didn't pay attention to what I was doing." Painful feelings can arise when we're clumsy, and that pain can inspire us to sharpen our awareness. In that sense, mistakes are helpful. When we stumble, we need to pay attention to how we stand up, not just why we fell down. When we give our fullest attention to our life, we feel the joy of our unity with all things and people, the awareness of a unitary, complete presence. This joy gives us the motivation to pay attention. We learn to practice for its own sake, beyond ideas of gaining something, such as relieving stress or attaining happiness. Our days are then filled with calm attention and we understand what is meant by Buddha Mind.

Naturally, we're concerned with everyday attention, the kind we give to people, things, and our surroundings. But there's a more subtle concern that arises, the attention that we want to receive from others, when we feel the need to be noticed, to be accepted and admired, to feel important in the minds of others. A strong desire for personal attention is a form of suffering, the activity of a hungry ghost that takes us far from our original self.

How can we resolve this suffering? How do we let go of the attachment to gaining attention for ourselves? By turning it around, by giving attention. Doing so, we transform the desire to gain attention to directing our attention to the succession of present moments, orienting our mind away from desires. Most important is to pay attention to how we pay attention. So the ancient Zen master wrote, "Attention! Attention!"

When we sit in zazen, we notice when and how the mind wanders, when it stops paying attention to the breath and, as a result, becomes unruly. With attention to attention, we can return to our breath when we become aware of the wandering. Giving full attention to things and people is like keeping a large pot of soup on the stove for all who pass by to help themselves. If the temperature is too hot, they won't eat, even though the soup is nourishing. And if it's too cold, they won't eat. We need to maintain the right temperature to nourish our life and the lives of others. So we pay attention to our temperature: "Am I too hot, am I too cold?" With the right temperature everyone will be nourished.

Zazen can feel discouraging. Sometimes we lose our way. But even when we feel discouraged, we shouldn't give up practice. This is the key point. We continue practice beyond ideas of success or failure, beyond good or bad. We simply continue paying attention to things, to people, to ourselves, and especially to our attention. This is the best way to govern our lives.

Gift-Giving Mind

The Apple campus in Cupertino has created a Buddhism Employee Association that is related to its mindfulness program. An idea like this was unthinkable twenty years ago when I was presenting "Meditation at Work" programs for local companies and government agencies. At that time, corporate managers told me that meditation on the job would "put people in a zone" where they would lose their creativity and ambition. Today executives realize that meditation relieves stress *and* increases productivity.

Mindfulness practice can be the starting point for developing a deeply inclusive orientation toward life. It can become more than a technique for achieving something, such as relief from stress. Committed practice opens us to selflessness and the intention to live life authentically. Following morning meditation, Zen students silently renew this commitment. Without it, mindfulness by itself loses its appeal.

When we begin Zen practice, we may feel that zazen is something we do only for ourselves, and tend to practice only when it's convenient or helps us feel comfortable or when we're in the mood or feel anxious. In other words, it can bring physical and mental comfort. But life is a gift to share, not a commodity to keep for ourselves. We have to let the gift flow, to pass it on. Zen practice emphasizes continuation and return of the gift of life.

When we sit down in zazen, we're not limited by our physical body. We become Buddha's unlimited body. But this can only appear when we have gift-giving mind, when we understand our inherent gift-giving nature. *Gift-giving mind* appears when we feel gratitude for the gift of our life. Gift-giving mind impels us to pass on the gift so it can continue. Efforts based on this gratitude express our true nature. We create life each moment with this original giving mind, letting life flow and continue. Without unimpeded gifting, the flow is hindered. We become confused and create problems. With a gift-giving giving mind, we feel our inherent creativity that is always fully functioning, in the smallest of activities.

When people think of death, they usually believe they will lose something personal. Seeing life and death this way is the greatest cause of human suffering. We can't feel free if we think our death is a personal loss. Freedom means we're always ready to pass on this gift of life, and continue gift-giving mind.

According to Zen practice, everything is Buddha nature. When we understand this truth, we trust our original giving nature. We are ready to practice giving, because everything is fundamentally the same. Our practice is the expression of our inherent enlightenment.

Off with Their Heads

Interview with Travis Marsot

Travis Marsot is a biomedical engineer working on medical devices with Auris Surgical Robotics in San Carlos. He is in his early forties, married with two daughters. He began Zen practice in 2014 and was ordained as a Zen monk in 2016.

Teresa Bouza: How did you become interested in Zen and how did you start to practice?

I grew up in Iowa with a lot of self-determination and individualism in my upbringing. I played competitive tennis, and my first priority was to become self-sufficient in a material sense. When it came time to choose a career, a lot of opportunities seemed to be out on the coasts. My wife and I made it to California, and after many years I got the project I had always wanted.

I was at a Shins concert—they're a rock band from New Mexico—and I was explaining to a friend how it was all working out for me. I'd gotten this project; I just had to deliver. The last song of the concert, called "Sleeping Lessons," had a verse that went, "And if the old guards still defend, they got nothing left on which you depend, so enlist every ounce of your bright blood, and off with their heads." The moment they sang "off with their heads," I felt completely destabilized. I wasn't there; my "head" was gone. That was September 2012. I tried to understand the experience. Having been so focused on advancing my sense of self—my career, my job, my family—I slowly came to see a bigger world. I had imposed limits, a framework that allowed me to be effective, but only in a narrow sense. That glimpse was a spark and it gave me the opportunity to see the world in a new light, although at the time I didn't know what to do with it.

When I was younger, I read David Foster Wallace and thought a lot about the state of the culture, where things were going with technology and materialism and the burgeoning of narcissism. We grew up in the same neighborhood, and I'd developed this innate trust in his voice. I found a commencement speech he gave called "This Is Water," and I listened to it over and over. It was a message about not going too far down the path of intellectualism, about trying to be compassionate. He says you can have a liberal arts rationalization for everything, and with that attitude, you'll go through life a slave to your head without realizing these are just default settings. I believed him when he said you have to work hard to get beyond self-interest. I knew I was self-centered and limited in how I could care for others. My daughters were getting old enough to where that kind of view was starting to matter. They'd look at me and I'd feel them thinking, "Are you going to be here for us?" That was a big part of my motivation to start spiritual practice.

You come to Kannon Do almost every morning. Do you find it challenging to keep the practice and your family life?
I just do it. It's a priority for me. I don't want to miss a day.

Do you feel that self-observation helps you operate in the everyday world?
When you're checking in with yourself, you can see patterns and feel rhythms in your life more easily, and so that observer sense helps a lot. You see your activity more clearly. I can also sense

what others are feeling and what their motivations are. I can focus my attention more completely on other people.

When I first came to Kannon Do, Les told me, "We have such a cultural need to be productive." That struck me: "Are we productive to the extent that we never exist naturally anymore, forgetting just to experience life as it is?" Once you remember who you are, it opens up so many possibilities.

How has practice helped you in your work?

Here's an example. Last week, I asked for a promotion. I'd never done that before. It may sound counterintuitive, but after a stretch of meditation, I knew the timing was right. I knew things weren't working well within our team structure. I laid it out and said, "I think I deserve a promotion." I started into what I wanted to say and was surprised to observe that I wasn't anxious.

Is there anything else you'd like to talk about?

I see a culture emerging out of Silicon Valley. Our world is increasingly decentralized. Technology is playing an increasing role in our lives. Where the twentieth century was framed by giant towers of finance, the future is going to be more about interconnectivity. People see Buddhism as one of the highest achievements of eastern civilization. In the technology boom we're living in, there's a new interplay between East and West and the potential for a new culture that values mutual respect and embraces change. Buddhism emphasizes sincere effort and kindness. It's an important source for cultural character building that, if we're to evolve, we're going to need. I'm optimistic it will happen here.

The Problem
of Excitement

To fully appreciate life, we need to express ourselves in the simplest, most straightforward way, doing away with clutter and not allowing ourselves to be distracted by what is not immediate. If we do this, we'll see more clearly, without distortion or confusion. This also means letting go of the anxiety of craving for things we don't have and the excitement it generates in us. We might come to Zen practice looking for excitement, such as gaining wisdom, increasing mental powers, or learning something unique in order to feel and appear special. But the quiet practice itself is inherently unexciting. By its nature, it doesn't create stimulating experiences. Its expression in our body and mind is subtle; there is no obvious or noticeable payoff. We are just alone with our mind, and it might feel as if nothing is happening. For many people, that can be discouraging: they came expecting a tangible result. If they do not drop that expectation, they will not stay with the practice very long.

Someone who was about to stop practicing meditation told me, "I need to get on with my life." I asked what he meant, and he answered, "I don't have time to sit." I didn't think that's what he meant. I suspected he found zazen boring, preferring something more entertaining. We are captive to excitement, but if we can stay with the "boring" feeling for a time, we may come to recognize our attachment and begin to be free of it. When we don't understand how our mind makes judgments, based on biases and preferences, and how it makes up stories to justify such discrimination, we will have a hard time with spiritual practice and with everyday relationships.

Gambling is a big industry in this country. With few exceptions, when casinos are built they become popular and financially successful almost immediately. For the amateur, gambling provides a high level of emotional excitement. It promises the chance of "winning," not just cash but the feeling of being a "winner." The excitement of taking a risk and creating something new provides much of the motivation in the high-tech world. And we may feel some excitement when we first start meditation practice. But if we maintain the anticipation of obtaining something from our practice, the meditation hall becomes a casino and when we don't experience a "payoff," our attitude becomes, "I'm out of here. I won't spend any more time at this table."

When a well-known spiritual teacher gives a talk, many people attend and some feel excited about obtaining new knowledge or insights. But will they continue their spiritual practice the next morning? After the excitement, then what? Will they look for more excitement, or learn to practice without such anticipation?

People new to Zen practice often feel that zazen is boring, that it does not provide excitement or entertainment. But when properly understood, "boring" is the most important quality of zazen when we understand that it really means a mind uncluttered by desires, free of a preference for excitement. When we let zazen be *as it is*, we can see what's going on in our mind, the subtle states and activities we're not normally aware of. But when the mind is busy trying not to be "bored," it can't be informed. "Boring" mind is like the calm surface of a pond that accurately reflects what appears before it. If we are willing to stay bored, we can see how our mind wanders and what it wanders toward. Then we have the opportunity to wonder, *Why does my mind go there? What about this distraction appeals to me?* The boring quality of zazen enables us to discover the irritant, the root of anxiety. So boring is actually a great gift. Through it we can appreciate the quality of practice and life. We should keep our practice ordinary, without ideas of excitement.

The Meaning of Zazen

In Zen Buddhist monasteries, attending meditation periods is not optional. Rarely do monks linger at the sound of the bell, and the discipline in the name of pedagogy can be harsh. Senior monks criticize young monks when they make a mistake. Badgering and tough discipline are considered the best ways to teach students to pay attention and do things well. This approach does not work well for Americans, however. We are used to the comforts and distractions of the modern world. Suzuki-roshi saw that American students need to be encouraged, guided without critical demands placed on them, while leaving them to decide for themselves the best way to practice in their particular situation. He felt that changing the early-morning start time to make the practice easier for Americans would be a mistake.

Zazen before dawn is traditional. It is a quiet time—the engines of modernity and even the sounds of the natural world have not yet begun to rev up. American lay practitioners have to consider how they can fit meditating that early into their lifestyle, with jobs and family responsibilities. It's a *koan*, forcing individuals to reflect on how valuable the practice is to them, how vital it is in their lives, how much comfort and convenience they're willing to give up, what accommodations and negotiations they're willing to make with their families and bosses.

Beyond such logical considerations is the feeling dimension. As it says in the "Song of the Jewel Mirror Samadhi,"⁸ "The meaning is not in the words, yet it responds to the inquiring impulse." We are all inherently spiritual beings, but the strong energies of our intellects and egos often block this recognition. When we do get a glimpse, it awakens the "inquiring impulse," and we want to know more. This is the starting point of Zen practice.

At Kannon Do, we continue the practice of 5:30 a.m. zazen. On average, ten people come to sit, sometimes as many as twenty or as few as two or three. We recognize the challenge for people with busy, committed lives, so we suggest to individuals who can't come at that time every day, that they try to come once a week, or once a month, or once a year. Everyone is encouraged to make accommodations in their schedules to underscore the priority of spiritual practice in their lives.

Why the emphasis on predawn zazen? Why is this important? In part, it's to teach self-discipline to young monastics—mostly in their teens—to help them let go of comforts and attachments, to help them mature. However, beyond its function for building character, it has religious meaning. It means sitting in meditation before problem-solving or analytical thinking kicks in, before the mind has become engaged in the busy affairs of everyday life, a time when it's most open, ready, uncluttered, when the mind can subtly discern its absolute nature and feel the fundamental divinity we share with all things. It's an ideal time for the deepest expression of our spiritual nature.

Sitting in meditation at dawn provides a sense of being born with and, simultaneously, giving birth to a new day. There is a feeling of our turning darkness to light, and a perception of the inherent unity of everything. The mind becomes pliant and responsive, ready to face the day with equanimity and confidence. The result is peace of mind and composure.

There is more to life than increasing its speed.

—MAHATMA GANDHI

Who Are Zen Students?

Eagerness and confusion were constant companions during my early days practicing Zen. I wanted to learn whatever I could, but the Buddhist worldview was elusive for me. Two conflicting remarks about Zen students exacerbated the frustration. I heard one Buddhist minister say at the end of his lecture, "Zen people are the cream of the crop." Several weeks later, I heard another minister, a likable fellow, full of good humor and candor, say, "Zen is for leftover people."

I wrestled with these statements for months, until finally I saw that the first minister was expressing respect for the practice and the concerted effort individuals make to seek the truth. He wasn't saying the individuals who practice Zen are somehow superior. He was appreciating the resolve and discipline needed to sustain the practice.

The second minister, I decided, meant you wouldn't be practicing Zen if you were not somehow discontent. Although some who come to Zen practice are successful in their work and family lives, they recognize a sense of incompleteness and want something deeper in their lives. Others are drawn to the practice because their lives aren't going well at all. They're unhappy, insecure, unstable. Some feel a sense of isolation, of being misfits. Others experience anxiety, grief, or fear. Still others lack confidence or a sense of self-worth. Whether seeking completion and wisdom or relief from suffering, when determination is aroused, we make an effort to bring practice into our lives.

Zen students make a serious commitment to practice, even during periods of discomfort and discouragement. At some point, they have to give up expectations of attaining anything and simply trust the practice itself, daily meditation, and the effort to be mindful of life. This is unusual in a culture that emphasizes goals and success. We live in a world in which traditions and values are changing at an unprecedented pace, and we feel unsure about the ground of our social and spiritual foundation. These are fluid times, when we question "truths" once firmly held, and individuals expand their need and their openness to explore deeper meanings.

All of us are capable of both confidence and confusion, of ambition and humility. We all have strengths and weaknesses, are capable of selfishness and selflessness, of doing good and causing harm. We can be wise as well as foolish. To face these crossroads is at the heart of the human condition.

In each of us, there's a tension between these two sides of our humanity. This conflict can be a constructive irritant with the potential to wake us up to fundamental questions about life and how to live authentically, opening the door to spiritual searching to discover the source of things and the meaning of our life. We come to practice seeking the truth of existence, hoping to resolve questions that have troubled humans since the dawn of consciousness: *What is the nature of the world I live in? What is the purpose of my life? How then shall I live? What is this sense of unease?* We are concerned about cruelty, greed, war, and indifference to the suffering of others. Even if the religious traditions of our childhood no longer inspire us or provide us with answers, we seek to resolve such questions in the spiritual realm.

Our seeking is made increasingly urgent by the pressures, distractions, and speed of daily life that leave no respite from anxiety. Thich Nhat Hanh tells a story about a man and a horse: "The horse is galloping quickly, and it appears that the man on the horse is going somewhere important. Another man, standing alongside the road, shouts, 'Where are you going?' And the first man replies, 'I don't know! Ask the horse!'"

There's a growing concern that we're moving too fast, holding on for dear life, not understanding where we're headed. The increasing pace of change forces us to move faster to keep up, to create even more change. The lack of stability in our daily lives and the accompanying turnover in personal and social values cause us to lose touch with our essence—who we are most deeply. The resulting confusion may cause us to feel like "leftover people." But when we make the effort to regain our balance and find our true self, we become "the cream of the crop."

That's What Zen Will Do for You

Interview with Victor Legge

Born and raised in London, Victor Legge was introduced to
Buddhism at the age of nineteen. He lived at Buddhist centers
in the north of England, before moving to the United States
in his early thirties. Now, thirty years later, he's married, has
a teenage daughter, and teaches mathematics at De Anza
College in Cupertino.

Teresa Bouza: How did you become interested in meditation?
In 1971, I was nineteen and quite unhappy. I had an experience
with LSD; I realized that there's another reality to life, that I'd
been asleep. I saw thoughts as just thoughts and that I could separate myself from my thoughts. It was a way out of my misery.
Then a friend gave me a copy of *The Way of Zen*, by Alan Watts,
and meditation seemed to be at the core of the practice.

I practiced with different Buddhist groups in England, mostly
Zen. I liked the retreats. I felt more energized, less depressed.
Then, other emotional issues started coming up, and I was overwhelmed. I had no awareness of emotions except feeling bad and
feeling good. That's all I knew. I couldn't distinguish one emotion
from another.

Some friends went to America and lived at the Zen Center in
Los Angeles. In 1983, they invited me to join them, and I stayed at
ZCLA for seven months. It was a defining moment for me. Living
at a Zen center really changed me.

How did it change you?

After two or three months there, I had a feeling inside my body that I recognized as "contentment." I'd never felt that before. My normal state in England was depression. There'd be moments of happiness, but most of the time I was depressed.

After I left LA, I moved to Monterey and married a woman there. I couldn't find a Zen practice in Monterey, so I got involved with Landmark Education, the successor to the est training, a program that was somewhat controversial. In 1986, my wife and I had a big bust-up, and I moved to San Jose and found Kannon Do. I practiced at Kannon Do for four or five years, then left for more than a decade.

Why did you decide to quit your Zen practice? Did you feel it wasn't working for you?

I wanted to come every morning and found it difficult to do. I don't know why. I went to retreats, but it wasn't enough. I need a lot of structure. Coming to Kannon Do once every day was helpful, but I couldn't sustain it, so I stopped.

In 2000, I completed my masters degree in mathematics at San Jose State University, got a teaching job, got married, and then we had a child. When I came to Kannon Do the second time, my life experiences had grounded me—being married, having a child, having a full-time job I loved. It settled me in. Now I'm able to come every morning and it isn't difficult.

Do you think when we have difficulties sitting we should just still show up or should we respect that feeling and quit? And what do you think was the difficulty for you?

As a broad response, I think it's resistance. But unless you're desperate, you should always keep your word. I try to come to Kannon Do every morning. It's important to me.

What do you mean by keeping your word?
If you say you're gonna do something, like "I'm going to come to Kannon Do every morning," do it. Keeping your word to yourself and also keeping it for other people.

You said when you were nineteen you realized you were asleep. Can you elaborate on that?
When I took LSD, I didn't have hallucinations, just this awareness that I was asleep, that I'd been asleep my whole life. I also saw how easy it is to misinterpret what's being said. I would say something and see all the different meanings that could be interpreted from it. I realized how difficult communication is. To get someone to actually understand what you're saying is really difficult. That was a revelation to me. But most important, I had the feeling of being really alive.

What was that like?
Everything becomes vivid, and you realize that most of the time you're in your head, in a dream world, as though the world enters you through a cloud of thoughts and is always diluted. At ZCLA, I also felt truly alive. Being at meditation retreats also makes me feel alive.

Do you feel that after almost fifty years of practice you're not asleep anymore?
It's a matter of degree. I don't feel as alive as when I lived at ZCLA. While I was there, I was meditating in the morning, at lunchtime,

and in the evenings. But now, with a "regular" life, I'm almost always looking for entertainment—TV, Netflix, even a book. We get obsessed with being entertained, and to me it's about running away. Around 2000 and 2001, I had my child, and that was really good. I loved looking after my daughter. It was one of the greatest experiences of my life.

You mentioned that when you first discovered Zen, you felt depressed; you were dealing with certain issues. Have you overcome those difficulties or are you still working on them? It's a lifelong process. I still have a lot to work out, especially my anger. But I now have a lot of structure in my life. I'm with people all the time. I come home, there are often people staying there, there's always stuff to be done. Structure helps me a lot.

Breakthroughs also happen. You're going along and suddenly your life changes. My health is better, I have more energy, more money, and I feel smarter. That's what Zen will do for you (laughs).

When I started practicing Zen at nineteen, I was too young. It's good to have some life experience before you take on Zen. I've gained a lot from being married, having a child, and having a job.

Your confidence builds over time, you feel more settled. I noticed that at ZCLA, the people who seemed to get the most out of Zen were married and had jobs. The people who were kind of messed up didn't seem to get as much out of it.

Why would that be? There's a lot to be said for life experience. Buddha was married and had a child. He had life experience before he started practicing. I think the combination is good.

Do you feel now, after so many years of practice, you're able to bring your practice outside the zendo, sustaining your awareness throughout the day?

I have to make a conscious effort. If I'm at a traffic light or walking from one place to another, I have to intentionally focus on my breathing. When I give zazen instruction, I tell people to do that. Like, when you're walking to the bathroom or from your car to the office, focus on your breathing or your feet stepping. Personally, I have this resistance. I'm in love with my thoughts; I think about a lot of things.

My energy levels are good, and I'm having a really good time. But there's so much resistance, even after all these years, to just let go of the emotions and distractions and just be in your body. For some reason, I'm still resistant to it, after all this time.

Do you think therapy and sitting are a good combination?

I've done therapy. I think therapy and sitting go well together. Meditation goes well with almost anything. We think so much. It's a perfect balance, especially in the West. Meditation is powerful in combination with other things, like running a business, being married, having a daughter. Having all that structure helps.

Do you see value in having a teacher?

I've never had a proper teacher. At ZCLA, there was someone I liked, who I wanted to be my teacher. I was thinking about asking him formally, but then I left. I have a thing about authority figures. My father and I didn't have a good relationship, and I had issues with my mother as well. I do think about it from time to time.

Maybe you'll become a Zen teacher.

People ask, "You've been practicing for forty-six years. How come you're not a Zen teacher?" I haven't really thought about it. I'm kind of rebellious. My dad was authoritarian and I didn't like it. When you become a monk, traditionally you submit to the authority of the teacher. It's authoritarian.

No Need for Cleverness

All live-born creatures emerge at birth from the safety and comfort of their mother's womb. Quickly they sense the challenges of the environment and turn instinctively back to their mothers for nourishment and protection. They stay in this dependent state for a period of time, depending on the species. Some are granted their independence sooner than others, depending on how long it takes their initial, fuzzy awareness to evolve into a clear perception of what will be needed to survive and to develop the problem-solving skills to avoid dangers and obtain life-giving resources.

All living creatures require these skills, a continuous awareness of what's going on in their environment. Depending on their capacity to be creative, they develop a degree of cleverness in applying their awareness and talents. We all share this aspect of cleverness, necessary for sustaining life. Because it is universal and impersonal, it is innocent. However, when greed arises, when we crave more than we need, it can turn into something else. A scheming cleverness, motivated by ego and self-aggrandizement, may provide what might feel like satisfaction, but which, in the end, brings us no joy.

To nurture our spiritual life, there's no need for cleverness. Intellect and knowledge are not even required to live authentically. This wisdom is available to everyone; it's not reserved for "gifted" people. Whoever we are, we can live in accord with the truth, without compromise, hesitation, or delusion. Zen practice is founded on the ancient insight that everyone is inherently enlightened and that everything we do is a manifestation of Buddha's activity, the worldly expression of our spiritual nature. Zen practice insists on using the energy, skills, interests, and intuition we already have. Rather than thinking, "I can't" before trying to do something, we can say, "I'll do the best I can."

To express our inherent spirituality, we must go beyond being casual in our attitude toward our life. We need a strong incentive to understand its meaning, to know the reason for our own existence. This is a serious matter, requiring that we abandon ideas of gaining something from the inquiry. Spiritual practice requires, first, that we pay attention, and second, that we not deceive ourselves. The modern world encourages us to maximize possessions and hit a home run with success. That orientation requires cleverness, always being on the lookout for opportunities for material or emotional gain, just as a cat silently stalks a bird. A life driven by a hunting mentality can never be fully satisfied; it will always feel constrained by its pursuit of possessions. Chasing after personal gain stands directly in the way of appreciating life. When we approach life as a spiritual practice, constraints drop away.

What does cleverness mean in the face of truth, transiency, and impermanence? Mistakenly believing that *things* in our life can be permanent, we pursue them with intensity. But when we loosen our grip and appreciate transience, we can taste the joy of mindful living. We will naturally give up the pursuit of excessive possessions, and understand the true nature of our life, as a skilled carpenter understands the material he is working with and goes with the grain. We too need to understand the nature of the material we're working with. We get splinters and stumble at the craft of life when we go against the grain.

Spiritual effort aims at balance in daily life, not huge spikes up and down, on and off, pulled this way and that by likes and dislikes. Letting go of scheming cleverness, we emphasize the unique and delicious content of each moment that is calling for our attention. Practice emphasizes heeding the call from within to do what must be done, to attend to what's in front of us, to be in sync with the call of the universe within and without. With this attitude, our mind becomes stable and balanced, pliable and present, accompanied by a feeling of inner warmth. This engaged attitude is independent of intellectual capacity or skill; it only requires self-trust, selfless determination, and appreciation of the ephemeral nature of things.

Dharma in the Ordinary

In the early 1960s, a young man sought out Suzuki-roshi. "I want to know about Zen. Can you teach me?" Suzuki-roshi replied, "We meditate at 5:30 each morning. You can join us." Six months later, the young man came again to Suzuki-roshi. "I've been coming to meditation for six months, and you haven't yet told me anything about Zen." His response was, "We also sit in the evening."

When we are new to Zen practice, we believe that it will provide something wonderful, something that exists outside of ourselves, which has been absent from our life. After practicing for a time, we see that there's nothing *external* to be gained, that we already are ourselves and always have been, only we just didn't recognize it. We realize that it's not just us, that everyone is special—in their own unique way. This realization brings a sense of well-being and freedom. We stop trying to attain something outside of ourselves, learning instead to experience satisfaction and fulfillment in the very activities of daily life—eating, sweeping, cooking, cleaning the bathroom, and being with people. What we once saw as ordinary *is* the expression of the Dharma, or Truth. This recognition and acceptance makes life less complicated.

Most people view their lives through the prism of self. They worry they won't get what they want, are in turmoil trying to get fame and affirmation, feel anxious when problems arise, and ask, "Why do I have to suffer?" We think and feel this way when we're convinced of our own importance, when we see ourselves as a prince or a princess. Like royalty, when our desires aren't met, we act as though the world has conspired against us. When we let go of the notion of our own importance, we experience profound fulfillment in ordinary activities. There is no longer anyone important nor anyone not important, and we're free to engage playfully in the world. This understanding is not intellectual; it derives from the wisdom of direct experience and a fluid mind that observes things as they are.

Through Zen practice, the anxieties of self-importance and personal ambition are transformed into the peace and confidence that arise with humility. We understand and accept that no one is more special than anyone else. Each person has her own skills, talents, history, imperfections, and challenges. These traits often make us feel separate from each other. When we see that they are ordinary, shared, human qualities, when we stop making judgments, we see that our foibles actually unite us and we approach each moment of life as a beginner, without an agenda. We stop feeling pressure to prove our specialness through competition and acquisition. We enter each moment as a novice, filled with anticipation, recognizing that no one is an expert at being alive. Holding a sense of importance or expertise creates an expectation that the world will acknowledge, respect, and praise us, and when that doesn't happen, we get angry and create our own suffering.

As we learn to do things with a mind of nonattachment, without desire for particular material or emotional payoff, our *doing*— whether it's physical labor, creating art, solving a problem, or relating to people—will naturally express the highest quality we're capable of. We will find satisfaction in everything we do. Rather than raise problems of specialness, we would be wise to find our true self in selfless ordinariness. Our inherent enlightenment is expressed when there are no strings attached.

You Just Have to Care
Interview with Scott Williams

Scott Williams is a software engineer at Google. Married, in his thirties, he grew up in a family that was interested in Eastern spirituality, and he started reading about Zen as a teenager. After moving to California in 2010, he found a Sangha and a teacher. "My reading in high school indicated that in order to do this Zen thing seriously, you need a teacher and a Sangha. Those were two things I didn't have access to growing up in a small town in Colorado. Without them, it's difficult to practice on your own," Scott said.

He finds meditation especially useful when things get stressful at work. He sees many people in Silicon Valley finding relief practicing mindfulness, even those who aren't really focused on spiritual development. "It is like an appetizer for the spiritual development that might come for them later, maybe in another lifetime. I definitely see it ease their anxiety."

Teresa Bouza: After starting Zen practice, did you notice any change in how you deal with situations at work?
I remember a lecture at Kannon Do about taking care of everything. It doesn't matter if we're taking care of trees or people; we give them both the same respect and consideration. This is the fundamental belief behind the modern environmentalist and animal welfare movements. And it especially applies to our jobs.

We spend half our waking lives at work, so bringing the practice of caring for all things into the workplace means you approach all aspects of your job with the same care that you approach meditation and gardening. I find that to be tremendously helpful. It keeps me from feeling overwhelmed, increases the quality of my work, and makes me a more reliable person. Taking that kind of care has given me a reputation for being trustworthy that I didn't have when I started work.

At work, I'm often with people who are far more intelligent and have much stronger opinions than I do. When they disagree with me, it can be difficult not to take it as a personal attack even though we're both trying to create the best experience for the user. It takes courage to be humble about your beliefs. That's where meditation practice helps, because it's a training in letting go. It can be difficult when the stakes are high to let go and try to understand the other person's words without letting your ego take over. It doesn't always work, but the humility and openness we learn in meditation practice helps.

You're a manager now. How do you balance the pressures of work and family with the commitment to a spiritual practice? It can be a challenge. I try to see my relationships at work—even the most tense conversations—as opportunities to practice. Having a performance discussion with someone I think needs improvement but who doesn't agree with me is a conversation that could go south pretty quickly. People think Zen is pacifism, letting yourself be pushed around in the interest of preserving peace or not causing violence. I think Buddhism is about not getting buffeted by your own ego. When you disagree about something that matters, Zen training allows you to refrain from reacting to affronts people might hurl at you so you can focus on what's important. Then it's not just the strongest personality who wins, but the person who's right. That requires getting out of your own way, and Zen training can be very helpful.

It must be difficult to stay calm when in the midst of heated conversations at work.

Exactly. There's an expectation at my workplace that the more senior you are, the more skilled you're supposed to be at peace-making. It's easy for someone in a leadership position to create trouble with one misplaced word. People look to you for direction. They watch you for cues. You define the culture. If you want a culture that's calm and based on the merit of ideas, you have to be calm and value ideas, and that's not always easy.

Especially when you're focusing on what's best for the user or customer.

My team has some strong personalities. They're wonderful people, but they have intuitions of their own that aren't always right, and some of them aren't reflective enough to realize that their intuitions aren't always correct. It can be difficult to reason with them, because to them it's just obviously true. It's a hard argument to have when you're trying to appeal to what's best for the user.

Is that what you are working on, being assertive without being confrontational?

I'm working on that in all parts of my life—my personal relationships, my relationship with my wife.

Do you feel that by practicing meditation, you're able to develop the confidence to be assertive when it's appropriate?

It helps. Learning through zazen that discomfort isn't going to kill you helps give you the confidence that the discomfort I have to go through in a disagreement isn't going to kill me either. That

PARALLAX PRESS

Find the latest news, author updates, and special offers at:

parallax.org
facebook.com/parallaxpress
twitter.com/parallaxpress

Please send in this card to receive a copy of our catalog. Add your email address to sign up for our monthly newsletter.

Please print

Name_____

Address_____

City_____ State_____ Zip_____

Country_____

Email_____

PARALLAX PRESS
P.O. Box 7355
Berkeley, CA
94707

confidence comes from practice. Looking at every conflict as an opportunity to practice mindfulness is helpful, intentionally trying to apply my Zen training in the moment.

When you sit on the cushion with a conflict in your mind day after day, you end up by seeing the truth.
I think so. As you find your brain drawn over and over to an argument you had at work, you wonder, "Why am I so stuck to this? Why is it following me around?" Then you see, "Ah, my ego feels threatened. If this other person is right, then I must be wrong. There must be something wrong with me." But that's not so. It's not either/or.

I'd say the biggest impact Zen practice has had on me is the ability to be with people who are suffering. I've gotten a lot of feedback as a manager that one of the things people value most is just being listened to. That's a real practice of mindfulness in the moment, because listening is a profoundly active experience. You can't just be nodding your head and waiting for them to stop. You have to be reflecting on how they're feeling and what this experience is like for them in order to empathize. As a manager, I find that my advice often isn't needed. People come to the right conclusion on their own just by talking it through. It's interesting that you don't have to be an expert, or pretend to be an expert, to help people. You just have to care.

And not be judgmental.
Exactly.

Is there anything else you'd like to share about your practice?
As a result of the practice and the teachings at Kannon Do, my

house is a lot cleaner and my desk is a lot cleaner. The emphasis on doing things well, with consideration, makes a difference in the joy I get out of my life. It's nice to come to work and even when you have something really boring to do, like expense reports, to make yourself a cup of tea and say, "The work I undertake today, I undertake for the salvation of all beings." That's a profoundly positive statement, and it's true. That's why I'm here. I'm working on expense reports, but there's something bigger behind this, and I take great pleasure in paying attention to those moments. That's what life is made of.

Natural Way
of Life

When Westerners hear about Zen practice, it seems both profound and exotic. We're drawn to its literary and philosophical erudition and also its lean and essential expression in art and culture. But as we become familiar with the practice, we discover that it's not at all mysterious, that the main point is simply to be ourselves, not the embrace of an esoteric way of life, but a return to our original self within the very life we're living.

We avoid being ourselves. We've become attached to ideas about who we're supposed to be, and we try to act "natural" from that place. This only creates complications and prevents us from actually being natural. Our natural way of life precedes any ideas about natural or unnatural. We need to go back before questions and answers, when the mind is unattached and free.

We understand life by engaging in life. So, in our practice, we rely on experience rather than intellect. There's no need to seek or hope for special experiences. Instead we emphasize presence, full involvement in ordinary, everyday activities, just as they are. Whether what takes place pleases us or not, it *is*, and from that stance we cannot but accept what happens. Through acceptance, we can give our full energy and attention to another person or an activity, without holding back. By loosening the hold of habits of resistance and avoidance, zazen helps us cultivate an accepting mind.

We are emotional creatures. We feel strongly about events in life—when a child is born, when we fall in love, when we're disappointed, when there's a serious illness, when someone we care for dies. In the midst of a world with ups and downs, our practice modulates the impact of emotions that might otherwise distort our experiences by rationalizing, justifying, intellectualizing, or playing mental games.

For almost everyone, practice starts with a vague feeling in body and mind. The Buddha and Dogen used this feeling to seek for answers. Zen practitioners in today's world are seeking for clarity, not a simple recipe to calm unrest, but to see clearly and accept what appears naturally, without interference. We don't know when something will appear, but timing need not be a concern. We practice without an agenda or a schedule. Searching this way raises questions that only we ourselves can answer. We resolve such questions by allowing the inquiry and unrest into our experience and accepting them.

When I started practice, I wanted teachers to answer my questions. But their answers were indirect, and I felt disappointed. Because I trusted them, I continued to practice, and eventually I understood that seeking explicit explanations was counterproductive. I saw that the teacher's role is to provide encouragement and let the answers appear naturally. Kobun Chino-roshi's motto, a summary of the Zen orientation to life, was: "Don't Worry. Don't Grumble. Don't Explain."

Although we may need help from time to time, the difficulties that appear to us are ours, and with practice, we perceive what's happening as neither good nor bad, and just take care of each situation. When we feel stress, we just sit with the dilemma and allow it to come and go according to the body's rhythms, without interference from our anxious mind.

Our practice helps us let go of preconceived ideas about truth, happiness, and even ourselves. Holding such fixed views is the way we try to control our life and others. But this only reinforces the ground of anxiety. Buddhist practice is to express "no-mind," understanding ourselves through experience, unfiltered by intellectualizing. This way, we feel oneness with *everything* and discover the inherent freedom of our natural life, including difficulties that may arise.

Did You See
the Gorilla?

Zen discourages the hyperdramatic and instead brings us back to ourselves in ordinary, down-to-earth experiences. Zen practice encourages us to open to whatever is happening in the present moment and observe whatever comes into awareness, whether products of mind or appearances from the world around us. Zen warns against distractions, noting that they might disrupt the mind's engagement in creativity or problem solving. But since distractions are inherent in the flow of thoughts, feelings, and impulses, how can we stay open to the flow of consciousness while guarding against distractions?

Several years ago, psychologists from Harvard and the University of Illinois conducted an experiment to test the premise that people believe they will see what's in front of them simply by opening their eyes and looking. Volunteers were shown a video of two teams of people passing a basketball and were asked to count the number of passes. In one version, a woman walks through the action in a gorilla suit for about five seconds. In another version, she walks through with an umbrella. The video was shown to several groups. After watching the video, volunteers were asked, "Did you notice anything unusual or odd?"

Half the people did not see either the gorilla or the woman carrying an umbrella. To them, anything that did not help the difficult task of counting the number of passes was simply not seen. The gorilla and the woman carrying the umbrella had been filtered out, since noticing them would not have helped the task of counting passes.

There are times in our lives when the intensity of the task in front of us requires us to give it 100 percent of our attention. Distractions, by definition, disrupt what we're trying to do. But some spontaneous arisings in the mind can be important and should not be ignored, such as suddenly recalling an important piece of information or an upcoming engagement, or having a sudden insight. Zen practice asks that we enhance our capacity to be attentive so that we don't ignore anything, while at the same time recognizing the difference between a distraction and useful information, and responding accordingly.

Zen practice is focused on the task at hand, but not so rigidly that the mind becomes closed to new information that may arise. It is like trekking up a mountain along a steep, rocky, narrow trail. We have to be carefully attentive to the stony, slippery path underfoot but also be aware of the steep side, the trail ahead, and the weather. Or like driving on the freeway, looking straight ahead and staying aware of our speed and the distance between our vehicle and the one ahead, while being ready to respond to traffic merging from an on-ramp. In situations like these, we may spontaneously see or hear or think of something that's useful or necessary for what we are doing.

Things that appear spontaneously in consciousness come from within the mind itself or are triggered by something external. It may be new information or creative wisdom we can evaluate on its own merits. But a spontaneous arising becomes a distraction when it sets desires in motion. Imagine a pro tennis player in the finals of a tournament, continually glancing at his proud and adoring family in the stands, basking in their smiles of admiration. By taking his eye off the ball, he takes himself out of the game.

Distractions become a problem when we can't let them go, when we assign them a level of importance that has no relevance to the reality at hand. There's no need to cultivate a samurai mind to stand guard against all distractions. We can keep our awareness in play, paying attention to whatever appears, and if it's not useful to what we're doing, if it's an expression of some desire, we should let it go. But if its appearance can help us with the task at hand, we should explore it. What's important is to keep a ready mind.

In zazen, we set aside expectations and simply let things come and go in our mind, acknowledging all of them. We do this by placing our attention on the in and out flow of our breath, unconcerned with what will happen next. When we can carry this orientation into daily life, the mind will accept the world as it is and not be tempted to construct a picture of how it thinks the world is supposed to be. Without holding on to expectations, we're simply aware of what we're doing, what's going on around us, and we're ready for whatever might appear.

Connecting with What's Important

Interview with Brenda Golianu

Brenda Golianu is an anesthesiologist and pediatric pain management specialist at Stanford's Lucile Packard Children's Hospital. She is also an associate professor at Stanford Medical School. Brenda was born in Romania, grew up in Canada, and attended medical school at Stanford. Now in her fifties, she's married with two adult daughters. She started practicing Zen Buddhism in 1987 and was ordained as a Zen priest in 2014.

Brenda developed an interest in religions and spirituality at an early age. She was introduced to Buddhism while still in high school, when she did a project on comparative religions. Years later she took a class in college and fell in love with the historical perspective on how Buddhism, Taoism, and Confucianism blended in China during the Axial Age. She studied Chinese and spent her junior year abroad in China, where she visited temples and traveled to Tibet. She became attracted to Zen while attending medical school. She liked the "simplicity, practicality, and no-frills directness." She found Kannon Do in the yellow pages of the phone book.

Teresa Bouza: Why is Zen practice important to you?
Zen has woven its way through my life for years. Practicing daily now, I feel grounded, connected with what's important to basic human nature. It's so easy to get lost in superficial things and lose

sight of the big picture. Zazen helps me stay connected to what I value, which is a sense of authenticity.

What's the most important thing you've learned in your thirty years of practice?
Be real.

What do you mean by that?
Be true to who you are. At the same time, when you meet people, it's important to meet them where they are, which can mean making adjustments.

Has Zen practice been helpful for your family life, your relationship with your husband and children?
Practice helps me enjoy others' company, because I've learned to bring my best energy, a kind of presence, without holding on to an agenda. These two things—presence and flexibility—have helped me become more skillful in relationships.

What do you mean "skillful in relationships"?
I listen better than I used to. I try to see from the other person's perspective, to put myself in their shoes. And I've become better at explaining my own viewpoint.

Are you able to pay better attention as a result of practice?
Absolutely. I'm now more aware and more mindful in varied activities. Sometimes we're mindful in one setting and then, when we change to a different one, everything goes out the window. Zazen practice helps me bring more awareness to each activity, to what I'm doing, and to consider whether there's another, fresh way to do something rather than repeating an old habit.

As an anesthesiologist and pain management specialist, paying attention and being present are obviously very important. How does practice help you to stay focused?

First is meeting the patient and paying attention to the person who's there for you to take care of. Sometimes you may be tired or overworked and feel you're not able to give the person your full attention. At moments like those, I stop and realize that I'm starting a very important activity with the patient, and I tune in to the patient's experience, what they're feeling, and cultivating compassion for their experience. Zen practice has helped me learn to feel the other person's point of view.

How are you able to maintain your Zen practice while attending to the demands of your family and the pressures of work?

That's an important question for anyone trying to practice who has other commitments. It's important to develop an internal compass that can guide you. "What should I be doing right now?" When I'm doing too many things, trying to be everyplace at once, I know it's a mistake. I try to decrease the extent of rushing around to be able to be more present and deeper with each of my commitments.

Is it a constant struggle to find that balance, or are you better able to achieve it now?

I'm finding a better balance now. I try to come to the zendo two to three mornings a week and to make it home for dinner most nights. I support whatever is necessary for my family's growth and development. And of course I respect my work time.

What would you say is the core of Buddhism?

For me it is compassion. I think it's compassion that allows you to make that link between people, between everything. That's the core for me.

What is the relationship between compassion and kindness?

Compassion doesn't necessarily mean being nice. True compassion can mean taking a firm stance, being very direct, if that's the necessary medicine. Determining what's most compassionate in a given situation can be challenging. You ask yourself what's best to do and then you figure out how to do it. Kindness can be important in terms of skillful means. Your message has to be delivered in the right way in order to be received.

What does it mean for you to be a Zen priest?

It's a commitment to future generations, to take the practice forward, to work on figuring out what Zen practice means for today's world.

What are you working on?

Society really needs this down-to-earth practice. I'm interested in figuring out how to make it more readily available to people, and more accessible. Zen practice has a lot of Japanese culture embedded in it. How do we adapt it to an American style of living while not losing the essence?

Is there anything I haven't asked that you think is important to mention?

Zen people tend to be serious; it's also important to have fun, to find joy in what we do. Sometimes we see the problems in society but not the opportunities for change and improvement.

Be patient toward all that is unsolved in your heart and try to love the questions themselves. Live your questions now, and perhaps even without knowing it, you will live along some distant day into your answers.

—RAINER MARIA RILKE

The Enlightened Mind

By exploring the workings of the human mind, the early Buddhist teachers were very much like modern-day psychologists, determined to understand how people create their own suffering through desires and attachment to everyday phenomena. They recognized the ways in which the mind creates feelings of separation by seeing the world in dualistic ways, rather than with a sense of wholeness and wonder. Without relying on dogma or philosophy, they wanted to understand the human mind through spiritual eyes.

From this experience—and the teachings that subsequently arose from it—Buddhism tells us the ways to behave in order to relieve suffering. Through stories and poetic expression, it paints a portrait of how we should orient our state of mind, as in this example from the Dhammapada:

> There is no greater happiness
> Than the happiness of freedom
> From the bonds of error and hatred.
> So let us live happily
> In freedom and without hatred
> Amongst those who hate
> Extending our love
> Boundless and unselfish
> To one and all.[9]

Buddhist discourses provide a view of the world without delusion or hindrance, encouraging us to act and live according to the Truth. Those early Buddhists patriarchs were remarkable, their insights about people and relationships amazing, when we consider that they did not have access to social experiments or to studies that demonstrate how an individual's history can affect the mind's view of reality. They relied entirely on intuition, inherent wisdom, and sharing experiences with each other.

For Zen students, absorbing and becoming intimate with the early teachings brings great confidence. When joined with personal practice, they create a strong breeze that reveals spiritual understanding by going beyond the screen of appearances and emotional concerns.

In the early days of Buddhism, if someone's mind was deeply troubled, it was said to be the result of past karma. Today, we seek more objective causes in the role that past experiences have had in creating present suffering. But whether suffering results from the karma of a previous life or from the trauma of our more recent past, Buddhism emphasizes that it is the individual who has full responsibility for regaining clear orientation of mind, and that our delusion is to be overcome by determined study and practice.

Zen does not rely on special techniques. Rather, it emphasizes selfless, spiritual practice to bring understanding and relieve suffering. Practice starts with slowing down our activities, both physical and mental, creating the possibility to relax body and mind in order to learn about oneself. There we have the opportunity to reorient our worldview from *self* to *other* and discover our inherent sense of reverence.

Affirmation

During a Q&A session following a lecture, somebody asked: "What should we do with a mentally ill person?" It was not a medical question, inquiring about therapies and medicines that can be effective treating a troubled individual. It was a religious question, asking us to go beyond a scientific "how to" for curing an illness and to consider our own attitude in relating to an unhappy person. If our attitude is one of caring—rather than indifference—our first step should be to reframe the question so that we can view it in a way that avoids negative labels that tend to isolate, stigmatize, and are also hard to remove. From a spiritual, rather than a medical orientation, the question becomes: "How should we respond to someone who is out of harmony?" To an individual whose life is out of balance, we should try to be as present as a mother is to her baby.

An infant disrupts our routine with its constant needs and demands and its inability to express or take care of itself. The caring mother does not isolate the child out of frustration or impatience; she instinctively knows how unnatural that attitude would be and how it would lead to suffering. So our attitude must start with self-lessness directed toward someone who is not in harmony. It is part of the responsibility we have toward each other.

The orientation of spiritual practice is outward, toward "other." If our attitude is toward ourselves, it will encourage the separation and isolation that we want to avoid. If we turn away from someone who is out of balance because we feel uncomfortable or feel that engaging with him is "too much trouble," we create disharmony. If we say we care, then we need to explore our outward-facing orientation.

Zen master Dogen dramatically and precisely expresses a fundamental principle of the nature of existence, of our relationship to each other and all things that guide the spiritual life. In a story introducing one of his writings, he relates that the layman Sotoba had a profound understanding of the truth while hiking in the forest and composed a poem to illustrate his experience. It begins, "The sound of the valley stream is his great tongue, / The colors of the mountains are his pure body."[10]

Nature is seen here to have human attributes, meaning that nature inherently affirms our life. It explains why we love nature and why we want to be close to it and preserve it. At the same time, this poem shows that we humans affirm nature, that our life affirms the lives of others, and that lives of others affirm our life. However, if the mind is too logical, too self-concerned, it will be confused by the metaphor. About such individuals, Dogen remarks, "It is regrettable that many only appreciate the superficial aspects of sound or color."[11] Here we have the basis for the spiritual life, the understanding that our relationships are inherently affirming, beyond the superficial sensations of our senses.

Every one of us is out of balance sometime in our lives, temporarily out of harmony, temporarily "mentally ill." But most of us have the resilience to come back to balance and to continue our lives in relative harmony with society. Others are not so fortunate. Harmony eludes them; they spend much of their lives in isolation. Our job, our practice, is to affirm life as we meet it. When we encounter isolation, we try to encourage harmony. If we do not know precisely what to do, we experiment; we intuitively try something. When we feel out of harmony, that is, when we are "mentally ill," we quiet our mind and return to balance.

We are affirmed by all things. By extension, all things are affirming all things. This affirmation is not passive. It is continuously active, continuously practicing, like mountains and rivers, continuously aware of what is going on, continuously engaged. The Zen practice of bowing to each other, known as *gassho* in Japanese, is an expression of affirmation; in this act, we are not passive or indifferent; rather, we fully connect. In this way, by giving up attention to our self for a few moments, we discover the joy of being with the other person, without concern for like or dislike. As Suzuki-roshi said, "Sometimes we may bow to cats and dogs."[12] In the same way, we should be ready to bow to everyone.

Sitting in meditation with others is an act of affirming one other, with acceptance, without judgment. Being together helps dissolve any sense of isolation, a problem of the modern world. Great benefits have come into our lives through technology, but in our excitement to embrace it, we don't recognize how it can isolate us. We have to reflect on how to use our technology, consider when we use it, where we use it, and its value in that moment, measured against its impact on our relationships with each other. In the same way, we should reflect on how to use our life. Do we want to encourage harmony or isolation? Do we want to be active in the continual affirmation of all things?

When we meet a difficult or out of balance person, our practice—our inherent nature—demands that we become spiritually creative, that we find a way to affirm that person, as the starting point of taking care.

Soul-Searching

Soul-searching arises when we're confused, uncertain what to do with the life we've been given. We are trying to understand the meaning of our lives, who or what we are, what we believe in, what moves us. Mostly we are trying to understand how to live in a world that does not meet our expectations.

Our aspiration toward progress and technology is inevitable. It is inherent in the human species; it has existed throughout our history, beginning imperceptibly in the dim past with the first people, slowly gaining momentum over thousands of years as we became increasingly sophisticated with our lives and the world we live in. The modern, industrial, high-tech world emerged in parallel with humanity's changing orientation from ancient religions and obedience to a higher power toward the individual and the personal. People envisioned enhancing their intellectual, cultural, and material lives, finding the urge to express their individuality rather than submerge it, to explore what interested them instead of being governed by the church. For the past several centuries, we've struggled with adapting to individualism, materialism, and the pursuit of ideas and desires, leaving less and less room for the cosmic and the holy. Technology provides freedom to learn, new and higher standards of living, and improved health care. However, if it comes with risks and downsides and without the balancing influence of a spiritual worldview, it can become overwhelming.

Life based on a self whose main task is to pursue desires, even those that create progress, inevitably brings competition and destruction. Spiritual practice can help us modulate these desires and express them appropriately in the contexts of our families, communities, and nations, as well as globally. We can't support each other if we're consumed with our own needs and cravings. Recognizing the problem, we seek spiritual practice to learn not to be enslaved by desires. But even if we vow to live a disciplined life, the follow-through is never easy, as our minds are continually drawn to personal pursuit. It is vital that we break this tendency.

In traditional Buddhist practice, young people leave everyday life to enter the monastery, where they are trained to break self-centered habits. In the monastery there are no diversions, indulgences, or conveniences, leaving time only for the cultivation of an unselfish mind. Few of us today can, or want to, spend years in a monastery, so we are now creating places to practice in our own hometowns, places we can return to and rely on, where we can learn to let go of unmitigated desire and cultivate selflessness. When we make the effort to touch our true nature and not just our limited everyday self, Buddhist wisdom appears, everything returns to its essence, and we feel confident, joyful, and at ease. When we practice with humility, the teachings and practice become clear.

We try to maintain confidence in our practice, ever watchful for the arrogance that comes from the idea that we, personally, understand something, have attained something, or control something. This smug, surface kind of confidence is a dead end. Our confidence needs to rest on something deeply sustainable, independent of "personal" attainment. With that breadth of perspective, we have no trouble recognizing and avoiding being overtaken by selfish desires.

In the *Mountain and Waters Sutra*, Dogen writes, "The green mountains are always walking; a stone woman gives birth to a child at night."[13] The stone woman giving birth is the mind awakening to itself, its inherent enlightenment, going beyond the dead end of dualistic understanding—"this" versus "that"—and becoming alive. When we recognize that everything is giving birth continuously, we ourselves are giving birth to our true nature, and our soul-searching is over.

How Can I Help?
Interview with Paul Slakey

Paul Slakey is managing director of customer success with Vista Equity Partners, a technology investment company. He's been working in tech since 1984, when he got a job as an engineer with IBM. He is in his mid-fifties, married, with three children.

Teresa Bouza: How did you get interested in Zen and when did you start practicing?

In 1995, I was working for McKinsey & Company in LA, commuting two hours a day and feeling stressed out all the time. There was so much pressure to perform. So I started meditating in my backyard, just closing my eyes and trying to breathe quietly and not panic. After a while, I stopped, afraid I'd lose the competitive edge that's needed in the business world. Eventually, we moved back to the Bay Area and I took a few tech jobs. Then in 2008, I searched the Internet and found Kannon Do. I came to an evening meditation and talk and thought, immediately, "Doing it on my own is the hard way. This is great to have a community. I'm with others in the high-tech world who are also feeling stressed out."

I came back again and also started reading Zen literature. I found the combination of meditation and reading brought more calm to my life. I read about getting outside of judging and seeing different sides of a situation, and it just felt right. When a situation came up at work, I was able to notice a tiny gap that allowed me to pause for a second, and then respond in a useful way rather than just coming from fear.

It's hard to balance Zen practice with a stressful ten- or eleven-hour-a-day job. It's tough to meditate at 5:30 a.m., work until 7:00 or 7:30 p.m., have enough family time, and repeat it the next day. So now I sit at noon or in the evening and no longer at the center. I'd like to have less stress in my life and come to morning zazen. I miss the rhythm of sitting in the morning, but I'm just too tired at night, working that long—and the work emails are still flying in the evening. It's too much, which is a real shame. Our modern work rhythm makes you always connected. There are expectations we're going to be working even more hours than in the past, maybe than a generation ago. With the pace of life here, it's not easy to fit practice in.

Do you sit by yourself at home or in the office?
I sit at home. We have three cushions in the middle of the living room, a timer, a little incense, and a candle. Sometimes I sit by myself, sometimes with my wife.

Is the practice valuable for family life?
Definitely. It's not easy raising teenage children. There's one challenge after another, and our meditation practice helps us take a deep breath and say, "Okay, this is what is. How are we going to deal with this mindfully?" It's very helpful to have that grounding in meditation. When one of us is starting to lose it, the other can bring it back to a place where we're just being the observer of the situation and thinking, "Okay, what's the highest good here?"

Has whatever you acquired with the practice helped you manage teams differently?
Definitely. I don't know how much to attribute it to Zen and how much is my own approach, but I really approach work as, "How can I help? How can I facilitate the success of the company and others and see both sides in every situation?"

What reactions do people have when you tell them about meditation?
Most people seem kind of interested, but I don't know that it has a big impact on them. But a handful of people have come up to me and said, "I'm really, really interested. I was kind of looking for something. Thank you for sharing your story." I think that's how it is with Zen. It doesn't have mass appeal, but for a subset of people it can be really helpful. I guess the most powerful thing to do is to get the message out there, see who it resonates with, and encourage them.

Do you think it's easier to keep a competitive edge if you don't meditate?
Ultimately, I realized that was silly. I can practice mindfulness and be very successful at work. Meditation doesn't take something away from me. At the same time, I feel I can't afford to slow down. The pace here is fast, and I need to be good at my job. I have college-age kids and a mortgage to pay. So at least for now, this is a middle path for me—working hard and having meditation to help me *be*.

Is there anything else you think is important to mention for your story in the book?

I think the story hasn't been played out yet. For a while, I thought at some point I want to be ordained as a Zen priest. We'll see. Right now, I can't do everything I need to do at work and be a father and do what I'd need to do as a priest. My father was almost a Catholic priest. He went to seminary for six years of an eight-year program. Then he met my mother and decided not to become a priest, but he always had a very strong spiritual presence. My father's father, after his wife (my grandmother) died, decided to be ordained as a priest and went through the training but unfortunately by then his memory was so bad even the Pope told him, "You have to be able to remember the mass. If you aren't able to say the mass, we can't ordain you." My grandfather wanted to be a priest, my dad wanted to be a priest, and that same energy of wanting to serve and have a spiritual practice is in me and wants to express itself more. I can't do that right now, but we'll see.

Nothing
to Attain

In *Genjokoan*, Dogen writes, "When you first seek dharma, you imagine you are far from its environs. But dharma is already correctly transmitted; you are immediately your original self."[14] Zen Master Dogen is telling us that the dharma—the truth—is already in our hands, our mouth, ears, and tongue, in our skin, bones, marrow, and mind. If we don't understand this, he tells us, we're living as though we're separate from the truth of our own existence.

Truth is always present; we only need to grasp it. This, Dogen says, is the point of Zen. But we need to understand the concept of *grasp* from the standpoint of spiritual practice. Since we're inherently *not* separate from truth, there is no need to reach for it or actively try to grasp it. The dharma can't be grasped by clinging; it can't be grasped with our hands, eyes, ears, nose, or mind. And it can't be grasped by ideas or feelings. The dharma—the truth of our life—can only be grasped when we give up grasping and let the dharma fill us, without interference. Practice means letting the mind be open. We grasp the dharma when we let it express itself through our words and gestures, our actions and our thoughts. When we're driven by attaining something, the continual pursuit will bring on discouragement. The truth of existence is not a thing that can be attained. We practice based only on our trust of dharma, the truth.

Even though the body has physical limits, zazen posture expresses our inherent limitlessness. In zazen, we find balance and confidence through the depth and ease of our breath. This is how we appreciate our innate connection with the limitless world. In Zen practice, we simply allow the mind to return to limitless awareness, ready to acknowledge whatever appears.

Our greatest problem is the desire to control—people, events, and things. We do it because we misunderstand reality; we misunderstand the nature of life. Dogen writes, "A monk asked an old master, 'When hundreds, thousands, or myriad of objects come all at once, what should be done?' The master replied, 'Don't try to control them.... Even if you try to control what comes, it cannot be controlled.'"[15] Giving up trying to control does not mean retreating to a passive life. In a life based on practice, we focus on taking care. If there's a fire or a flood, we have to think in terms of controlling it, but our primary concern is actually focused on taking care of people, land, animals, and property. The same is true of friends, relatives, and those we meet every day. Even if they seem difficult, we can offer a caring mind.

Zen is a practice of nonattainment. We find rest when we're not caught by an idea of achievement, when we no longer feel we need to be in control. That is the practice of letting go, not holding on to ideas about success or failure. Letting go means to give up ideas about our self-image, about how we want to appear in the eyes of others. Our practice is to be aware of experience itself, to see clearly what is happening, how we're feeling, how things are working out. Honest awareness is sufficient. We don't have to classify our experience as good or bad. When we rest in nonattainment, we can enjoy all our experiences. Then the dharma is in our hands and in everything we do.

Planning the
Present

People living in prehistoric cultures were too busy trying to survive their harsh environments to give much thought beyond the present. Planning for the future is a distinguishing feature of the civilized world. We plan for the next hour, day, year, and decade. It is a necessary, reflective, analytical activity, required for the well-being of ourselves and our families. Planning improves lives, helps manage the problems of a complex society, and allows for innovation in the modern world. If we want something to happen in the future, we can plan for it. Successful school teachers prepare lesson plans, rather than walking into their classrooms cold.

But we don't always know when or where or how something will happen. There will always be surprises, a certain amount of imprecision in even the best of plans. Still, we can prepare mentally to take care of whatever happens. Spiritual practice covers that territory. It's a way to keep our mind ready, so even when we're taken by surprise, we're ready to respond.

Spiritual practice is a profound way to keep ourselves organized. It cultivates an expansive and accepting mind of wisdom, free of limits created by a demanding and anxious ego, allowing space for everything, known in Zen as "Big Mind." If the mind is not organized—ready for whatever enters our field of activity and consciousness—there's no room for creativity. Ideas get crowded out by the surging analytical activity. Planning needs quiet and reflection. Too much intellectual activity separates us from the present moment, causing us to lose sight of who we are and what we are doing. Organizing the mind in a big sense enables it to welcome and consider each idea. When every element of our well-conceived plan is backed by our ready mind, we'll have the confidence and know-how to take care of whatever happens.

Our life experiences can be a vital element for creating a plan, but sometimes a past experience will not be entirely relevant to a new situation. What was true back then may not be the reality we face today. So we shouldn't be too hasty in applying the past to today or tomorrow. We need *a ready mind* to show us how to use experiences appropriately.

Experiences are like stepping stones, helping us create a path to the future. But we need to recognize their relationship to each other so they can be wellplaced. It's not simply a matter of how well they fit geometrically; they rarely fit neatly like a jigsaw puzzle. Zen stone gardens are widely admired as works of art. The rocks appear randomly located in a large space, but they are placed to express something universal and natural. That kind of placement cannot be done intellectually or with an algorithm. The inspiring stone garden is created by a ready, meditative mind, beyond thinking, beyond planning. The care we take placing the stones of our garden is important. Well-placed stones are the work of a lifetime. With our ready mind, we are continually creating a Zen garden.

Zen practice requires the determination to live in the present, to be ready to respond to each moment and not be bound by images of ourselves, personal history, or others' ideas. To live in truth means not to be distracted by mental photos but to be who we actually are, not a fictitious personality of memory or fantasy.

We don't strive for perfection but to do the best we can with what we have now. And whenever we become distracted, our determination inspires us to return to the present moment and reorganize ourselves.

To plan our next move, the next phase of our life, it is helpful to not allow our mind to become too crowded. Then we can enjoy our life in a large sense. To enjoy life doesn't mean to accumulate emotional and physical pleasures, but to feel every moment and every experience as purposeful and sacred, including the unpleasant ones. When we can appreciate even difficult times, we can enjoy our life. The ready mind is the best way to appreciate everything, even when things don't go according to plan.

Zen practice is not about unraveling knots in our mind. It's about understanding that in Buddha's mind, there are no knots to unravel. Excessive mental activity can disturb the readiness of our mind and create knots. Our practice is to express Buddha's mind, especially when we have some confusion. It's about avoiding too much emphasis on success or failure, but expressing life as it is.

We would do well to forget about seeking special experiences, obtaining awakening—or indeed anything—from Zen practice. We can let our mind go beyond striving and be "organized" for whatever appears. Then we're ready to create something from the palette that is always with us.

The Power of the Practice
Is in the Streets

Interview with Randy Komisar

Randy Komisar is a partner with Kleiner, Perkins, Caufield, and Byers, one of the largest venture capital firms in Silicon Valley. He invests in entrepreneurs and helps them build businesses that can benefit the world. He started meditation and formal Zen practice in 1995. He is married, in his sixties, and is the author of the best-selling book *The Monk and the Riddle: The Art of Creating a Life While Making a Living*. He tries to bring his Buddhist values to Silicon Valley, a place he describes as "an extreme example" of the challenges people are facing all over the developed world, in terms of the frenzy, anxiety, stress, competitiveness, and uncertainty people are living with.

Randy has lived in Silicon Valley since the early 1980s. He says the world's tech mecca is now too focused on making money. He sees a lot of arrogance about that money. He thinks good things are being created but believes many products are "not interesting and have no real consequence."

He thinks entrepreneurs like Elon Musk represent the spirit of a past time when there were big thinkers who wanted to risk everything not to gain wealth but to test their ideas. "I do think there are people like Elon, but find me five others," he says.

Randy feels that operating in Silicon Valley while trying to follow the three essential elements of Buddhist practice (moral conduct, mental discipline, and wisdom) is like "going into the boxing ring with your hands tied behind your back." Despite that, he says one can still fight and make a difference: "I wouldn't do it any other way."

Teresa Bouza: How did you become interested in Zen?
I was exposed to Eastern philosophy and Zen through the '60s culture, with all its civil unrest and experimentation with drugs. I tried meditation practice at the time but was plagued by a busy monkey mind. Then mid-career, when I was forty or so, I felt disillusioned. I was successful but unhappy, which is actually a blessing. If you are unsuccessful and unhappy, you think it's because you're unsuccessful. But if you're successful and unhappy you have to look deeper. So I left my job, reopened to Eastern philosophy, and started my Zen practice. I haven't missed a day of sitting since. That was over twenty years ago.

What were you doing at the time you were successful but felt unhappy?
I was a serial CEO, and before that an attorney. I had worked at Apple Computer in its first incarnation. But I felt I was missing my life; it was moving so quickly and I was preoccupied with so many things that I found unimportant. My life was running by at such a rapid pace that I had no consciousness or appreciation of it. I was simply *doing*, I wasn't *living*. I had this gnawing sense that there was something bigger than success or accomplishment, though I didn't know what it was and or how to find it. I remember my first thirty-minute zazen sitting. I had a moment of what I would now call real awakening, and that taste was powerful. I had to keep doing it.

How did that change you? How after these twenty years of Zen practice are you different?

My values and priorities are clearer, I have a natural sense of equilibrium, I know what's important to me, and I don't easily lose my way. And more importantly, when I do lose my way, I find my way back pretty quickly.

Please elaborate more about these "values and priorities."

What I look for in my practice is peace of mind and a path to being the best person I can be. It's a sense of appreciating life and sharing it with others. An important value for me is non-separation, realizing my connection to everything. I find great satisfaction in sharing that sensibility with others.

Going back just to the period when you decided to start Zen practice and you reinvented yourself. Can you say more about that?

I love to create. I love innovation and I like working with others to build teams that can accomplish the impossible. I strive to construct healthy environments and cultures that can accelerate and amplify success. I have cultivated a role in Silicon Valley called "Virtual CEO," where I work through others to achieve more than I could on my own. To develop talent, not just businesses. That requires me to give up control, and effectively work through influence alone. Zen practice helped me feel comfortable with that role; not being in control, not owning the results, detached from the ultimate decisions, but at the same time being a curator of excellence. You have to be relatively selfless to follow that model, because it's not about you—it's about everything else.

What do you think about Buddhist ideas of renouncing family and wealth?

What's most powerful for me in Buddhism is what it brings to daily life. The power of the practice is in the streets—in daily life, in the communities where we live. The power is in *engagement*. My practice is translating what I've found in Buddhism into my secular life and expressing that to others through my behavior.

And you're in a position to make a powerful impact in the world.

Yes, I think that might be right. I've been privileged and that brings with it a responsibility to use that privilege for the benefit of others. In Silicon Valley, it's much easier to merge my practice and my profession than probably anyplace else in the world. Most businesses focus on extracting value—from the competition, from consumers, from other businesses—effectively living from some limited pool. But thankfully, I don't have to compromise my values or right livelihood by trying to extract value from someone else. I don't have to take; I can create. I experience abundance. And that's a privilege.

I don't want to be judgmental, but I just want to see if you think being a Buddhist and being financially successful is fine? What is your opinion on that?

I don't think you need to be an ascetic to live as a Buddhist. But I do think that to live right livelihood in the context of the Eightfold Path, you must be mindful of your consumption, what you take from the world and from others. I think of myself as a steward of the value I have created, not the recipient. Otherwise I don't think I could be successful in living the Eightfold Path.

What challenges in the world are you trying to address?
I'm most attuned to global education, food and nutrition, peace, social justice, and health care. These are the global themes that don't seem to change much from generation to generation. I gravitate toward people solving big problems that impact all of us. There's great consternation about how globalization impacts the world today, but there is no escaping our interconnectedness.

How long have you been in Silicon Valley?
Since 1983. I came from the East Coast, the Boston area.

You've seen a lot changes here. How do you see Silicon Valley now?
It feels troubled right now. It feels rather dysfunctional to me. It doesn't seem sustainable in its current form. When I got here, there was a humility to the valley, fueled by optimism. There was a sense that you could create things that would change the world, and there was humbleness that it was just your job, it was what you did, and that you weren't anything special. That's all changed.

There seems to be a new sensibility arising here in Silicon Valley about more and more people caring about mindfulness and Buddhism. I wonder if this could be the beginning of something.
Mindfulness is commonly taught as a tool, not a spiritual practice. Young people come to it either because they are looking for relief from what ails them or because they are looking to improve performance: to be smarter, more attuned, more acute. The mindfulness trend feels faddish to me. It doesn't require much commitment, and as a result I don't think there's much staying power to it. But as an opportunity for people to taste

awakening as I did the first time, it certainly creates a bigger funnel. I don't think we will see a huge transformation in sensibility from the mindfulness trend alone, but I do think we will see more people find their way to Zen practice as a result of experimenting with mindfulness.

A state that lets you rest in your own specific gravity and where you are not a subject matter but sit in your own nature, tasting original tastes as good as the first man, and are outside of the busy human tamper, left free even of your own habits.

—SAUL BELLOW

Zen and Character

A new Zen student asked me, "What brought you to Zen practice?" I answered, "I didn't want to be a jerk anymore. How about you?" He responded, "I used to be an assaholic."

In the United States, Zen has been popularized as though it were a commodity, a technique that alleviates stress, reduces pain, improves productivity, and is "cool." But the most vital aspect of this ancient spiritual practice is overlooked—its potential to build character.

In his 2015 book, *The Road to Character*, *New York Times* columnist David Brooks profiles individuals, who, over a span of centuries, inspired others with their contributions to addressing humanity's needs and aspirations. Included are Dwight Eisenhower, Frances Perkins, St Augustine, George Eliot, Samuel Johnson, and Dorothy Day. With grand eloquence, Brooks describes them as wanting "to live in obedience to some transcendent truth, to have a cohesive inner soul that honors creation and one's own possibilities."[16]

Brooks selected these individuals for the work they did on themselves to develop their strength of character. He writes, "They were acutely aware of their own weaknesses. They waged an internal struggle against their sins and emerged with some measure of self-respect. And when we think of them, it is not primarily what they accomplished that we remember ... it is who they were."[17] He adds, "They practiced a mode of living that is less common now."

Brooks sees a diminishment in the American character over the past several decades, a sense of modesty and humility being replaced by self-importance, resulting in a "superficiality in modern culture" because "we've accidently left this moral tradition behind." Describing individuals who do uphold the moral tradition, such as those profiled in his book, he writes, "You come across certain people who seem to possess an impressive inner cohesion.... They are calm, settled, and are silent [even] when unfairly abused."[18]

A strong sense of character is available to everyone, not just a relative few like the leaders described in Brooks's book. We can develop it by honestly accepting our weak points, by not denying them or becoming defensive or blaming others when we err. As Suzuki-roshi is quoted in *Crooked Cucumber,* "I think it is almost impossible to change your habits. Even so, it is necessary to work on them, because as you do so, your character will be trained and your ego will be reduced."[19]

Zen practice developed as a way to cultivate character in the lives of its monks. It starts with the erect posture of zazen, kept straight by "putting your shoulder blades in your back pocket." The upper body is open, held with confidence to allow the breath to come and go unimpeded. The mind makes its best effort to remain aware of whatever arises. When discomfort shows up, the mind does not immediately seek comfort, emotional or physical. We ask ourselves, "Can I sit with this for ten seconds more?" Then, "Can I do it again for another ten seconds?" If the pain or intruding thought becomes so distracting that we cannot sustain awareness, only then do we shift posture.

Dogen told his followers, "To study the Buddha way is to study the self. To study the self is to forget the self. To forget the self is to be actualized by myriad things."[20] He encourages us to face what comes to mind, what has been beyond consciousness, held out of awareness. With this stance, an increasingly confident mind lets go of desires and expectations, and finds selflessness.

The Freeway Always Clears Up
Interview with Jean-Louis Gassée

Jean-Louis Gassée worked with Steve Jobs at Apple, where he played a major role in the development of the Apple personal computer. Before joining Apple, he worked at Hewlett-Packard in France from 1968 to 1974, where he was responsible for launching HP's first desktop scientific computer and the development of its sales organization. From 1974 to 1978 he served as the Chief Executive Officer of the French affiliates of Data General and Exxon Office Systems. He writes *Monday Note,* a weekly blog exploring technology and business. He is married with three adult children.

Teresa Bouza: When did you start with Apple?
December 12th, 1980. I signed my contract the day of the IPO (initial public offering).

How many years were you with Apple in France?
Until I moved here in May of 1985.

What happened when you got here? I believe you mentioned that at one point you were the president of the product division, right?
Yes. That was toward the end. I was initially hired as a vice president of product development. I'm a college dropout from Orsay University in Paris. When I saw my father leave home between two *gendarmes* (police officers), I dropped out of the polytechnic and similar engineering schools. So I had no formal training, but

I had ideas about what Apple needed to do in France.

I landed in Cupertino in May of 1985 as vice president of product development. At the end, yes, I was the president of the product division. I remember when I was made president I had to dodge the heavy traffic on De Anza Boulevard to go into the executive suite.

It was a painful time for me because I was unhappy. I was probably "wrong" to be unhappy. People would have killed to have a job like mine, but at the time I couldn't be at peace.

When I started my own company in 1990 I was happier and I slept a lot better.

You had a very intense life. How does Zen fit into all this? When did you discover Zen?
I had a good therapist, Carlos, who told me I should meditate. We had two cushions in his office. I tried meditating alone at home. It didn't work. Then Carlos told me, "Look, you might benefit from joining a group. There's one in Mountain View." I said, "No, no, no." He said, "Okay, okay." He's a therapist. He can play the piano without looking at his hands. I was impressed. So I joined our friends in Mountain View.

That was 2005 and that was what I needed. Meditation came easy after a while. Of course, now people ask me, "Why is it easy?" I say, "There's no explanation." They asked me, "How should I do it?" I said, "Just sit. If you sit every day, it will come to you. You will find your posture, you'll find your breathing, you'll find ways to let your thoughts rise like smoke in the morning. It will come to you."

I was raised as a Roman Catholic. When I was about ten years old, I was a failing student. I was sent to this boarding school, which saved me from my crazy parents, but they did a good thing.

I have a debt to them. I look at my life as a long, long, long procession of people I can bow to in gratitude.

My parents were crazy, but incompetent as they were, they had the good idea of sending me to this Roman Catholic boarding school. The prefect of discipline was a geek. He was interested in electronics. Boom! My career choice was made. The whole religious ritual of Roman Catholicism, I had six years of that. Some of the ritualistic aspect ....

You didn't feel comfortable?
No. No. I respect it, but it's not my cup of tea. I like sitting.

Don't you think that maybe the ritualistic part emphasizes the sacred nature of what we are doing when we sit or the spiritual nature?
Spiritual, yes. I have nothing to say about sacred.

I prefer poetry like that of Ryokan, this Zen monk who writes about his isolation in winter, the wind and the trees and then going down to the village to beg and get drunk and roll around on the ground with kids, playing with kids. That speaks to me because it's not intellectual. It's poetry that pierces through some veil of mystery.

How did your Zen practice change you?
It changed me, and people around me, and my family. It made me calmer, happier. Also, I look at people differently. I've learned to listen differently. That has changed a lot for me.

Don't think. Try not to think. Trust your brain to process things. Just listen and also watch your stomach muscles. When people want to say something, you will see people consciously do this and stop in the middle of what you are saying and just say nothing.

A small epiphany from a Zen practice is that the freeway always clears up. What difference does it make? Not much, but instead of going mad, you can be merely frustrated. There is a big difference between frustration and going mad, getting in a rage.

What do you mean by that exactly, when you say that the freeway always clears up, that problems go away?
No, problems don't go away, but they don't become overwhelming, they are just there; they don't clog you up.

Do you have any major realization in your practice?
It just made me calmer. I am looking at things differently. Also, it has an effect when it comes to compassion, especially compassion for bad people. It's easy to have compassion for nice people. Forget that. Anybody can do that, but having compassion for truly bad people, annoying, bad people, it takes something. It doesn't mean approving or condoning.

Did it also help you to have compassion toward your parents?
Yeah. It's including compassion for myself because if I don't have compassion for myself, there's no way. You know the oxygen mask metaphor. You've got to put the oxygen mask on yourself first before you can help others. It starts with compassion for oneself.

Would you say that before you started Zen practice, you were not compassionate? Were you too tough on yourself, blaming yourself for everything?
Yeah. I still do that, but it's always a question of degree and how much it takes of your own inner life. In the current political

climate in the United States, it's very easy to seed anger, but then what? "This guy is an ...!" What does the anger achieve? Actually, it prevents me from achieving things.

What do you think attracted you to Zen practice?
I knew that there was something in Zen for me. I knew it because of course in France, Zen has a reputation. It is part of the vernacular as in a certain form of quiet, calm posture. And because I was agitated, that certainly was attractive to me.

So you are not a religious person. You're a spiritual person.
Yeah. Of course, we're spiritual.

Do you think your practice made you connect or have a sense that there's something bigger, that we are part of something bigger?
That's a mystery to me. Why we're here, why we can have something that I don't think other animals have, which is the self-awareness or being aware—that's a mystery. There are libraries full of exploration and discussion of why we are spiritual beings.

What does it mean for you, being spiritual?
It's a good question. It means that we are not just mechanical. But I don't spend too much time on that because my observation is that we haven't made any progress on that. Maybe, just forget it. Live, sit like the old monk. Well, when I'm hungry, I eat. When I'm tired, I sleep. Of course, I also believe that our job as humans is to know the world and prostrate ourselves in front of the wonders of the world. I also believe that. That's probably the closest, truest, simplest expression of my own spirituality. My job is to

adore the world, which is why sitting is the easy part. A very flowing, clean part of the job description.

That can be an inspiration for people listening to that.
Well, I hope so. My life is too idiosyncratic.

What do you mean?
At one point in my life when I left my parents' house, I could have become a petty criminal. I had several opportunities to do that. When you work in bars and restaurants and street clubs as I did, there are plenty of opportunities to become a petty criminal. It didn't happen. Probably my genes. I spent a lot of time on couches. The good news is it gave me an appreciation for people's difficulties.

Do you wish you had started Zen practice earlier?
Sure. I would have made people around me a lot happier. Yeah, I wish I had started much earlier. You know *ex post facto*, replaying the movie.

Maybe if you were to be a manager now you would be a different one?
Yeah, because I used to be an angry man. I stopped running like a mad Frenchman thanks to meditation. People notice that in the office where I work as a venture investor. After I had started meditating, my mentor said, "There's an imposter in the office. He looks exactly like you. He really looks like you but he's not like you." Zen calmed me down.

Is That So?

Zen Master Hakuin lived in Japan in the late seventeenth and early eighteenth centuries. He is said to have created the now-famous question, "What is the sound of one hand clapping?" Hakuin believed that the understanding arising out of practice in everyday life was deeper than the understanding that comes from practicing in the monastery, since lay people faced more distractions, held more responsibilities, and experienced more heartbreak than the monks, and so needed to practice with firm diligence.

Hakuin was greatly respected and had many disciples. At one time in his life, it is said that he lived in a village hermitage, close to a food shop run by a couple and their beautiful daughter. One day the parents discovered that the young girl was pregnant. Angry and distraught, they demanded to know the name of the father. At first, the girl wouldn't confess, but after much harassment, she named Hakuin. The furious parents confronted Zen Master Hakuin, berating him in front of all of his students. He simply replied, "Is that so?"

When the baby was born, the family gave it to Hakuin. By this time, he had lost his reputation and his disciples. But Hakuin was not disturbed. He took delight in caring for the infant child, obtaining milk and other essentials from the villagers. After a year, the young mother was troubled and confessed to her parents that the father was not Hakuin but rather a young man who worked at the fish market. The mortified parents went to Hakuin, apologizing, asking for forgiveness for the wrong they'd committed. They asked Hakuin to return the baby. Although he now loved the infant as his own, Hakuin gave them the child without complaint, saying only, "Is that so?"

We respond to surprises and disruptions in several ways, depending on the degree of inconvenience. When the telephone rings and interrupts what we're doing, we accept it with little protest. If we develop a flat tire while driving downtown, or the power goes out at home or at work, we might feel annoyed, but hold no residual anger toward anyone. When our car gets rear-ended or we get laid off from work, we probably experience negative emotions. When we can let go of them, we will have no problem. But when they remain, suffering arises.

Hakuin's story is about the mind of enlightenment, showing us how equanimity can be expressed in the midst of the surprises and challenges of ordinary life. It's a love story—without an object—a universal embrace of every situation, without judgment. It illustrates the mind of practice, of no attachments, and no "self" to defend, simply accommodation and taking care.

People come to Zen practice in search of an epiphany, some kind of enlightenment to feel special, experience excitement, or acquire power. They fail to recognize their purpose as just another effort at acquisition. Even if an exciting experience does occur, the basic unease is unaddressed. Although we believe we need to acquire things to gain happiness, what we really want is the flexible mind of Hakuin. Buddha's mind of no suffering embraces change without resistance because it understands the true nature of all things.

In his treatise on zazen, *Fukanzazengi*, Dogen advises, "Put aside the intellectual practice of investigating words and chasing phrases, and learn to take the backward step that turns the light and shines it inward." This admonition is not easy to put into practice; it requires complete dedication, a willingness to go beyond the thinking patterns and judgmental tendencies of our usual mind.

Look carefully at an image of Buddha, the half-closed eyes and slight smile expressing wisdom and serenity, a mind at rest. The straight back and head held upright expresses discipline and determination. The mind of a Buddha is already in us. Equanimity can help us in our daily lives amidst the most difficult surprises and disruptions.

Lost in
Transition

The 2003 film *Lost in Translation* is a portrait of disillusionment, disengagement, distraction, and separation. It portrays two introspective, intelligent, good-hearted people who have lost their moorings spiritually and emotionally in a boisterous, speedy world.

Bill Murray plays the role of Bob, an aging actor on the downward slope of his career, yet still recognizable to the media and the public. The film opens with Bob riding through Tokyo in a taxi from the airport to his hotel. He displays no expression as his cab passes the tall buildings, flashing meganeon signs promoting this and that product, and the crowds of people surging toward the delights that downtown has to offer. In his hotel room, he sits on the edge of the bed, disinterested, not knowing or caring what to do next. The next day we see Bob unenthusiastically filming commercials for a high-end Japanese whiskey.

At the same hotel is Charlotte, played by Scarlett Johansson, a recent Ivy League graduate in town with her husband, a photographer on assignment in Japan. He's continually busy with his equipment, getting ready to rush off to work, paying her little attention. Bored and lonely, she sits idly looking at Tokyo from her hotel room window.

On a day trip to Kyoto, she comes across a Zen temple where she witnesses monks chanting the *Heart Sutra*. Their ceremony catches her attention. In the next scene, back in her room, she's on the telephone with a friend in the United States, shaking, and on the verge of tears. She tells her friend about the Zen ceremony, saying, "I didn't feel anything" followed by "I don't know who I married." Clearly Charlotte needs someone to talk to. Her friend, not hearing the cry for help, says, "Can you wait a moment?" We hear silence, then, "What were you saying?" Charlotte replies, "Nothing." They say goodbye and the chance for connection is lost.

"I didn't feel anything" comes as a surprise. Watching the Zen ceremony, her face showed that she *did* feel something. So what's happened? Charlotte's carefully constructed, habitual ways of seeing and feeling have been shaken. Witnessing the spirit of the ceremony, she saw something outside her usual confines. It threw her of balance.

Later, arm in arm with her husband in the hotel lobby, they run into Kelly, his superficial and immature starlet friend. She and Charlotte's husband chat, ignoring her until he finally says, "Oh, this is my wife Charlotte." When Kelly leaves, Charlotte is unhappy, having been left out. Her husband defiantly defends Kelly. "Not everyone can go to Yale," he says. They walk on, this time a few feet apart.

That night, both unable to sleep, Bob and Charlotte meet by chance in the hotel lounge. She asks what he's doing in Japan, and he says "I'm getting two million dollars to advertise a whiskey when I could have done a play." She tells Bob that she came to Japan with her husband because "I wasn't doing anything." When he asks what she does, she says, "I'm stuck. I don't know what I am supposed to be."

Later, walking together on the busy streets of Tokyo, they see Bob's face on a huge neon sign advertising whiskey. Everyone they meet—in the hotel, at the commercial filming, at a party—is all upbeat and engaged in their lives. Bob and Charlotte, by contrast, are without passion, barely alive. Like she says, they're stuck. Relationships with their spouses lack feeling, restricted to schedules, appointments, and home improvement.

Throughout the film, Bob's character is downbeat. He never smiles; his comments are clever, cryptic, and ironic but without real humor. When he confesses that he chose to give up the chance to engage in his life's passion for the sake of the money, we get the sense that he has been making this trade-off his entire life, following convention, rather than his intuition, thereby consigning himself to purgatory. Likewise, Charlotte's character—nice enough on the surface—is without joy. On three occasions, we see her being ignored or dismissed, twice by her husband, once by her telephone friend. She craves affirmation, but is denied it by the people supposed to be closest to her. As a result, she is lost.

Charlotte's character is a metaphor for the unhappiness created by lack of intimacy, the greatest of human needs. Intimacy comprises acknowledgment, acceptance, trust, love, and a sense of connection with others and with the world at large. Without intimacy, we are left with isolation and personal suffering. In our modern world, we are experiencing diminished intimacy and courtesy, creating anxieties and social problems. It is the downside of the growth of technology, automation, and global competition that emphasize efficiency and the speediness needed to meet shorter deadlines. We are allowing ourselves to be distracted, paying less attention to each other while keeping an eye and ear open for the message that might come through on our electronic device.

Bob and Charlotte start to share their stories and dreams, listening and laughing, as they develop warm feelings for each other. But when they eventually part, Charlotte is left to wander the crowded Tokyo streets waiting for her husband to return from a shoot, while Bob heads for the airport, back to his safe, comfortable, soulless life. The film is a poignant portrayal of how a sense of meaning can be eroded by ambition, materialism, and insensitivity, exacerbated by modern lifestyles and values. Viewers take heart, though, that Bob and Charlotte touched each other and had a glimpse of something meaningful.

Giving Up Toys

A man is talking to a friend on his smartphone while playing a game on his laptop. As soon as he hangs up, his wife, who has witnessed it all, proclaims, "How could you do that to him!" "What do you mean?" he responds, a little baffled. He thinks he was fully present for his friend. But is it true? How can we measure presence? Of course we can't, so it's important to acknowledge that there are levels of presence we are not aware of and that when we divide our attention, it's possible one (or both) of the objects of our attention is being shortchanged. To maximize our attention, and to be present with our friends and colleagues with respect, it is necessary to focus our attention by doing one thing at a time.

Computer games are filled with color, speed, and the need for agility and cleverness. Our mind is always on the lookout for attractive games like these, and we become attached to them, as kids get attached to toys. Infants like anything within reach. Small children become attached to games and dolls. Adolescents get attached to cars, music, clothes, and sex, at a certain age. Adults become attached to cars, music, clothes, sex, success, and even failure. Our old ideas and habits turn into attractive toys.

We come to Zen practice because we have doubts about ourselves and our place in the world. We confuse our larger self with our relative self and feel trapped. We have become addicted to ways that no longer serve us, and live without freedom or naturalness. Zen practice leads us away from habits, attachments, and addictions that are obstacles to our freedom, and turns us toward "readiness of mind." One way to do that is by giving up toys, no longer seeking for things outside ourselves to play with. When we give up attachments, we find ourselves.

To be free of habits is to be free of emotional toys, free of addiction to attractive features. We're better off enjoying the ordinary forms, colors, and sounds of the everyday world—people, animals, rain, flowers, the moon, and ourselves. Buddhism provides a perceptive, profound, and mind-altering insight into the true nature of the reality of life and of all material things. It is the recognition that every entity is inherently "empty"—not as in the emptiness of a water glass that is devoid of content, but that everything is:

- Transient—changing every moment, despite what our senses tell us.
- Temporary—does not exist indefinitely.
- Devoid of an essential self, or core.

When we recognize that all things, including ourselves, are "empty," then we will not feel addiction or compulsion.

To be free of toys means to understand the larger world of our true self, the unfolding world without permanent shape, form, or color. Understanding this is the basis of spiritual practice. Suzuki-roshi wrote, "If you understand yourself as a temporal embodiment of the truth, you will have no difficulty whatsoever. You will appreciate your surroundings and you will appreciate yourself as a wonderful part of Buddha's activity, even in the midst of difficulties."[21]

This is how we should understand our life—a temporary

manifestation of something vast, something greater than a separate self. To have this appreciation, we need to see both worlds, to see ourselves and others as colorful, playful, suffering, creative, loving, and unique, *and* transient, without separation, inclusive. Zen practice is to see ourselves as an expression of the world of emptiness—awake, perceptive, and not seduced by toys.

I Know the Work I Should Be Doing
Interview with Ken Simpson

In his seventies, Ken Simpson is an engineer—designing, programming, and supporting systems for the manufacture of semiconductors and wafers. He currently works for Western Digital in Fremont. He has four grown children.

Ken began meditation on his own when he was fifty-nine, and started formal Zen practice two years later. It was a difficult time in his life. He had a difficult boss. He says meditation helped him to decide to quit that job. He also credits his Zen practice for his increased sense of well-being and says, "Troublesome stuff doesn't get to me as much as it used to. It is a good feeling."

Teresa Bouza: How did you start Zen practice?
About twelve years ago. I was in a situation at work that I didn't enjoy. I was working for a fellow who was mercurial; his moods were all over the place. I was also going through some personal stuff. The marriage was breaking up. So there was a lot in my life that was not positive. I had a friend in grad school decades ago, who had taken some meditation classes when he was kind of stressed out, and he liked it. It seemed like it was working for him, and I put that in the back of my mind. I had come to realize that I was a lifelong seeker; I knew there was something I needed to find out about and wasn't quite sure what it was.

When I was stressed, a friend came to me and said, "Ken, you need to do something. You're acting a little erratic." He got me seeing a therapist who believed in the idea of observing what's going on. That was years ago. Today it's called mindfulness. I thought it would be a logical thing for me to start doing meditation, so I got some books about the mechanics of meditation. I was doing it at home for about a year when a friend who was coming to Kannon Do invited me. That was ten years ago. I was skeptical of organized religion, but eventually I came, and I'm still here.

In the beginning I had a sense that this is what I needed to find to resolve whatever my searching was about. I thought, "Okay, now I know the work I should be doing," meaning working on the self versus therapy or attending groups. And in the process of meditation, I came more in contact with who I am and I realized the job I had wasn't worth the money. "Why should I make myself miserable for money?" There was no trade-off. So I left the company, and I've never been sorry. I kept up my Zen practice. It has allowed me to stay calm or return to a calm position in times of turmoil. I don't mean I'm always present, but it's a place to come back to.

When I was younger, I would have periods when I was depressed. After a couple of years doing the practice, I never had another depressive episode. Five years ago, I was sitting in my backyard and I could tell things were starting to get to me. I was starting to slide off into the blackness. I was having lunch and I thought, "This is just like having a meal in the meditation hall during a retreat." I popped into that point of view, and I didn't get depressed, and I thought, "This stuff really works." We can talk about not having a gaining idea and other Zen principles, but the practice itself really works.

You left a job that made you unhappy after you started meditation. How did your practice help you to make that decision?

Throughout my life, the story I kept worrying about was, "I have a family, I have a home, I have a mortgage, I have responsibilities to take care of. So I need to continue the work I'm doing." Then it came to me that there are other places to work. I thought, "This isn't the only job, and I would probably be a better father and husband if I were happier instead of being depressed and under the weather." So I took nine months off and reentered the work force through contracting, instead of trying to find a permanent position. I realized I don't want to be a manager. I like people but managing isn't what I want to do. I like creating things.

When I got out of school I didn't expect to find myself in the business world. I studied photography for a while. I used to draw when I was a kid. I went back to drawing, and then I taught myself to paint. That's my real passion, doing art. It's something I need to do. I have a meditation practice, but I also have an art practice. It's something that allows you to discover yourself or to center yourself, basically what we do in meditation. Like meditation, it touches places I don't touch in any other away. Meditation is a "nondoing" activity, and nothing else in my life is like that. It's one way *to be* without having to try to be something.

Did you become an independent contractor after you quit your job?

When I went back into the field, I would go back for projects. I worked with systems and semiconductors companies, and that's what I am doing now at Western Digital. I was a contractor three years ago, and then they put me on as a full-time employee. I like project-oriented work—start something, finish it, and go on to something new—compared to assembly lines where you kind of do the same thing every day.

You said that after meditation without a gaining idea, you noticed you enjoy people more.

In my practice I haven't had any great realizations, but what I have is a growing feeling of well-being. Overall, my life is at a "more happy" state. I enjoy people much more than I did fifteen or twenty years ago. I like interacting, playing with them. People can be fun.

There's been a change for the positive. At one point before I got into practice, my normal mode was gray, afraid something negative was going to happen, and always feeling there were things I *should* do but I wasn't sure what they were. I'd catch myself driving to work with various voices in my head. One was a project manager saying what I had to deliver that day. That stressed me out. That was my "normal," and with meditation, the voices melted away. When I feel that way now, I know something's bugging me, and I can explore what it is. I don't feel on edge, or dread what's going to come tomorrow.

Has meditation also helped you to better manage interactions at work?

I was okay dealing with people before meditation. But I was having a difficult time with a person I was working for, and Zen practice allowed me to disconnect from him and leave after fifteen years working there. My practice has helped me navigate through job positions, being more objective whether the job is something I can enjoy, versus thinking, "I need to do this whether I like it or not."

Have you been able to maintain the practice?

When I don't feel great, I often realize, "I didn't meditate this morning." I've gone through cycles where I stopped meditating, but I always come back. I attend Wednesday nights when there's a lecture, and Saturday mornings when we work together to clean and maintain the center. And I always go to meditation retreats—I wouldn't miss that. Staying with the schedule keeps momentum.

You have been in Silicon Valley for quite a long time. Have you reflected on how people here could benefit from Zen practice?

One of our Sangha members who works at a high-tech company here in Silicon Valley described going back to the Midwest to attend a wedding, and the whole time he was away he didn't eat any food or sleep at all. He felt as though he was riding some kind of a high wave, that he didn't need basic nurturance. When he came home, his wife had to take him to the emergency room. I see how that can happen. There's so much momentum here, you can forget basics like eating and sleeping, or feel you don't need them. I was having kind of the same thing going on when I was at the job and then I started Zen practice and realized, "I don't need this pressure. I don't need this kind of craziness in my life." People think, "I need to keep doing what I'm doing or I won't survive, I'm not going to be successful." When you're in that state of mind, you can probably benefit from meditation practice, as I did.

What's in My Best Interest?

How we answer this age-old question will determine how we view the world, what we consider to be the truth, and how we respond to situations that arise in our lives. The unreflective answer might be, "My best interest is getting what I want."

If we have a change of heart and our world reorients toward others and the world around us, the answer might become, "My best interest is to be selfless." This attitude is a reflection of a wide and generous mind, a mind of strong character, willing to let go of its own desires for the benefit of others.

Suzuki-roshi came to the United States at age fifty-five, and just as the Buddha did ages before, he left a safe, comfortable life to share himself and his experiences with others. The practice and efforts of these spiritual leaders—one modern, one ancient—illustrate the depth of our innate capacity for selflessness and how it can take us beyond the usual notion of "What's in my best interest?"

The Buddhist precepts are based on the principle that living selflessly is in our best interest. When we hear or read them, and accept them as valid, guiding principles, we become inspired to live ethically, generously, and with discipline. But to live in accord with these principles, we have to go beyond acceptance and beyond *ideas* about selflessness. We have to go to the next level and *embrace* the precepts in our daily lives, leaving behind perceived limitations. Our practice is to embrace whatever comes, to embrace life without picking and choosing. Then there's no separation between us and the truth, and there are no regrets.

In a village in ancient China, a woman dies, and her husband's friends come to console him. They expect to find him mourning. Instead, he is banging on pots with a stick, singing. Shocked, they ask why, and he says, "I'm celebrating her." He is embracing her death as well as her life.

Zazen is silence of the mind, enabling us to see things as they truly are, to see what's going on, what is actually taking place, without an emotional filter or the distraction of habits and old ideas. This practice is the best way to understand what's in our best interest—in this moment and in the long run. With a quiet mind, undefended, we can see ourselves and recognize and embrace our whole being, warts and all—imperfections and undeveloped attitudes that without awareness might confuse what we think is in our best interest. We will never be perfect; so recognizing and embracing our imperfections is vital. This is spiritual maturity and the expression of the authentic life, one that has no interest in trying to fool ourselves or others. To actualize authenticity, we have to avoid becoming stuck in immaturity. As the New Testament tells us, "When I was a child, I spoke as a child, I felt as a child, I thought as a child; Now that I am become a man, I have put away childish things."[22]

To put away childish things is to be present in the reality of the moment, not lost in a made-up world. In a lecture in the mid-1960s, Suzuki-roshi quoted Confucius, saying, "The most visible thing is something invisible." Then he quoted a proverb, "The quiet firefly glows with light, unlike the noisy cicada." Both statements have the same meaning: to make a quiet effort without calling attention to ourselves. He encouraged us to do the important, fundamental work, even if others don't realize its value. Then, he said, "Our effort will not be for our self, but for our descendants." Suzuki-roshi concludes,

> This invisible effort will build up your character,
> and you will obtain the power to be a master of
> the surrounding. As long as you are chasing after
> just visible things, you will never understand the
> meaning of our life. This is how we devote ourselves
> to our way.[23]

Zen practice teaches us not to worry about being noticed or praised. When we bring our spiritual practice into our daily life, we derive satisfaction from our actions themselves.

A Comma in the World
Interview with Jayashree Mahajan

Jayashree Mahajan teaches managerial statistics, marketing research for decision-making, and international marketing to executive-level graduate students. She is in her fifties, married, with one adult son. Jaya went to Catholic school and over the course of her life has explored yoga, the guru tradition, Hinduism, and Buddhism. Her interest in meditation began after attending a talk by Indian philosopher Jiddu Krishnamurti when she was seventeen. She started meditation practice in 1987 and formal Zen practice in 2012. She believes her purpose in life is to be present for those who need her and to offer them something. Her Zen practice helped her through the sudden loss of one of her sons, who died when he was nineteen.

Teresa Bouza: Your encounter with J. Krishnamurti seems to have been important for you. Is there something particularly vivid that remains with you from his writings or seeing him in person?
I was particularly struck by his impatience. He pushed people right to the core, to cut out all the other things the mind does. To me, that aligns him with Zen practice.

What made you stick with Zen?
The message to pare down to the essence of what you need to be and do in life, which for me means to have your life be about others.

Can you talk about the loss of your son and how your spiritual practice helped you with that?

I lost my father at a young age and was completely alone and far away from where he was and unable to be there for the grieving process. That required putting the practice to work, realizing that if I sat myself down, I could deal with it. Life presented me with a learning opportunity, and it turned out to be essential for what I had to face later, when my son tragically passed away.

He was only nineteen, and the relationship we shared was rare. Then suddenly he died. A policeman came to the door and gave me the news. After the initial grief and shock, trying to figure out how to piece it all together, I insisted to my husband that we just sit, meditate, get the wisdom from within. That had to be the way. And a centeredness just came. I think it was because of the practice. It felt as though life had prepared me for this, and I was centered because people needed me to be. I had to put the practice to work, and that's what got me through. Because the practice kept me centered, I was able to write his eulogy, obituary, his service—these pragmatic things that needed to be done.

Were you able to heal?

We were able to heal because of the practice. I came to a place of understanding that this is what is. You can look at it in one of two ways. You can ask, "Why me? I just lost the best thing I ever had." Or you can say, "I'm grateful for having had such a unique relationship for nineteen years with such a beautiful soul. That was a gift to me." You go on, and you honor that every day.

How has Zen practice helped you with work?

I'm a professor in the business school at the University of Florida. I've always been trying to juggle a career with the things happening in my personal life. I'm dedicated to being a professional. I taught for a long time at the University of Arizona and the University of Florida. Now I'm teaching more online. How do I bring a sense of balance and perspective into the students' lives? I try to bring an attitude and demeanor of practice to the classroom.

I have to walk a fine line. I can't have them not be competitive, because that's the nature of the world they'll be functioning in. At the same time, every time I interact with them, if I see a level of honesty, because some people write openly and expose their weaknesses, I write back and say, "I really appreciate your honesty. I really appreciate you sharing the story," even though it may not reflect as well on them. The way I try to bring the practice into my work is to encourage people who are in completely competitive environments to be a little gentler with themselves and with those around them.

What about other values, like thinking about the greater good rather than just about their self-interest?
The focus of the class I'm teaching now is how American businesses can be more competitive in international markets. How can US businesses go overseas and be successful? One of the areas I cover is what I call the "bottom of the pyramid," the BOP market. There are more than four billion people in the world living on less than $3 a day. Many great companies have developed an innovative product that they take to the BOP at an affordable price. Because of my practice, I'm cognizant of doing things for the greater good, and the students enjoy discussing it. Even if just one person stops and thinks and maybe changes their way of doing things, I feel gratified.

Being aware of people who have a lot of needs in the world, and accepting responsibility.

Accepting responsibility is huge. A lot of people are not willing to be honest about or take responsibility for their failings. Among MBA students, there's a kind of bravado. You want to put your best foot forward, but you have to be able to acknowledge what you can and cannot do, and I feel that there isn't the acceptance to do that. It's kind of a cultural thing.

Do you try to communicate your Buddhist principles?

Yes, I do. It isn't easy. In business school, students are taught to be everything we wish they weren't. They're taught to be competitive and cerebral and not to use their inner judgment, their intuition. I try very hard to bring in those values of just thinking about the other person, the larger context, being honest, taking responsibility. There's only so much I can bring to the table, and I am okay with that. If I can bring three or four things to them, I think it's better than not doing anything at all.

You have had a lay ordination ceremony. Did you want to bring your practice to the world after that?

I've thought a lot about this. Over the course of my life I've been pulled in many directions, and I often think about my purpose in life. I jokingly say that this life of mine is a comma, a resting place. There are a lot of people I interact with who are just trying to cope. I feel like I need to be there as a comma, a pause in that world. Maybe at a train station, a bus stop, in my class, anywhere I can, I try to be a comma. This is something I need to be, my way of interacting with the world.

People come out of nowhere who have something happening

in their life, and I happen to be there at that moment, and able to offer them something. It's amazing. Over and over I experience this. That's how I live my life. I've lived in so many places in four different countries. I'm here now for who knows how long. Each instance there is something I can offer, and that's how I'll live my life.

Wow Moments

During the question-and-answer session following a lecture by Suzuki-roshi, a young man asked him, "What qualifies you to teach us?" Suzuki-roshi replied, simply, "I have some experience." I was *wowed* by his straightforward answer; there wasn't a trace of pride. He said nothing about personal success, his impressive credentials or experience, knowledge base, or insights. I heard in his answer that there is a way of learning beyond collecting information. It's about paying attention, allowing events to create experiences that become absorbed in body and mind. He was telling us, I believe, that we learn from the reflective, subtle side of our nature, not (just) our intellects.

Recently, a student asked me, "What's the most important thing you've learned in fifty years of Zen practice?" I said, "I'll have to get back to you." It was a profound question. Reflecting on it, I recalled one lesson that arose repeatedly over the years. In my early Zen readings, I came across the saying, "Religious awakening occurs by chance." I thought it meant we are given one chance, and if we miss it, awakening will simply pass us by. This random possibility, not within our control, proved, I thought, that life is unfair. Over time, my understanding has changed.

In 1958, I got on a plane in San Francisco and by chance, saw a young woman sitting by the window. Immediately I knew I had to meet her; it was a *wow* moment. Without hesitation, I sat down next to her. Mary and I have been married now for almost sixty years. A few years later, I picked up a friend's Zen book by chance and was immediately struck by this new way of seeing and the promise of freedom it held. Another *wow* moment. That's when I started practice.

Buddhism tells us that everything changes. It means there are new possibilities in each moment, *wow* moments waiting to be born if we're ready to discover them. We have to pay attention, set aside our prejudices and preconceptions, and be willing to engage our instinct and intuition. Zen practice helps us see the possibility of *wow* in each moment. After that, it's up to us.

When you meet the love of your life or discover a great universal truth, those are *wow* moments. But most awakenings are less dramatic. They are inherent in the texture of our breath, the chill we feel on our skin, fallen leaves, silent commuters on the train, the crunch of celery, the laughter and music of carpenters as they build a house, sunlight reflected in a puddle. Paying attention to all of life gives us a chance to be awakened by the ordinary moments of a changing world. *Wow* moments occur when we give life our full attention.

I have measured out my life with coffee spoons.

—T. S. ELIOT

Epilogue: Technology Needs a Partner

If you were raised in or near the neighborhood of the Judeo-Christian tradition, you cannot easily forget the Adam and Eve allegory portrayed in the Old Testament. Branded as "original sin," Adam and Eve's disobedience of their maker's instruction not to partake of the tree of knowledge became and remains the source of human suffering through successive generations. Lacking discipline and restraint, the first humans succumbed to their greed, thus losing the utopia of Eden for themselves and their offspring. They were not told of the negative consequences arising from giving in to desire, from ignoring this subtle dictate of wisdom. They were simply given an instruction to follow, not always the most effective way to encourage desired behavior. The inexperienced, naive couple did not take the warning seriously.

Many centuries later, in another part of the world, the Buddha discovered the same truth, not through admonition handed down from on high, but rather through his own personal searching: suffering arises through greed and ignorance. However, unlike the biblical legend, Buddha's understanding of the human condition does not envision us to be hardwired to suffering because our first ancestors were thoughtless, too casual about what was in their own best interests. Rather than a permanent "original sin," we inherited "original foolishness," a treatable condition, if we can be serious and attentive to the dynamics of our nature. The Eightfold Path specifies how we can avoid being seduced by the many attractive apples of this world and the unintended consequences of desire. Specifically, the teaching encourages us to retain the character and discipline to keep in mind the ethical practices of:

- Right View
- Right Attitude
- Right Speech
- Right Conduct
- Right Livelihood
- Right Effort
- Right Mindfulness
- Right Meditation.

To lead a righteous life—to treat ourselves, each other, and our environment with attentive care—is, in Buddhist understanding, the antidote to desire and foolishness.

This formula has not been taken to heart on a scale large enough to help the world. Not much has changed since the authors of Genesis recorded what was going on with people and how they get themselves into trouble. In an interview on CNN on September 10, 2010, well-respected theoretical physicist Stephen Hawking told television host Larry King,

> *Mankind is in danger of destroying ourselves by our greed and stupidity.*

During a follow-up interview with King six years later, he said,

> We have certainly not become less greedy or less stupid.

And he warned,

> With advancements in technology, there are new ways
> things can go wrong.

He was referring to the powerful technologies of the last eighty years or so. Despite the promise of benefits professed by scientists and futurists, including extended life spans, treatments and cures for stubborn diseases, and improvements in the quality of life, Hawking's negative assessment has supporters. Bill Joy, cofounder of Sun Microsystems, introduced his famous article in *Wired Magazine* in April, 2000 this way:

> Our most powerful twenty-first-century technologies—
> robotics, genetic engineering, and nanotech—are
> threatening to make human beings an endangered
> species.

Technology has been the key to the progress and improvement of the life of mankind. The scientific revolution of the sixteenth and seventeenth centuries brought new knowledge, clearing away unexamined beliefs about the world. In the mid-eighteenth century, the industrial revolution saw machines starting to do the work people had been doing by hand, increasing productivity, economic activity, and availability of the material goods people wanted and needed. Technology has improved the standard of living in the developed world not just materially but also in medicine, food, and sanitation. Yet despite such advances, the world is still not at peace. Nations, tribes, enclaves, and individuals continue to squabble and threaten each other with harm, even annihilation; hunger and poverty continue while the earth becomes more polluted, without an end in sight.

Something is needed to balance the "progress" of the past five hundred years. To provide what the world really requires, technology needs a partner. That partner is our spiritual dimension, the mind expanded beyond logic and rational thinking, embracing its intuitive capacity and arousing its inherent wisdom. It is not "otherworldly"; it is accessible. Its mother is awareness—mindfulness of ourselves and what we are doing; its father is the continued determination to be authentic in relationships, to create meaningful, intimate, intentional bonds with people, things, and the environment, without being so overwhelmed by visions of "progress" that we lose our soul.

In his 1999 classic, *Ethics for a New Millennium*, the Dalai Lama argues that we need to understand what makes people truly happy by recognizing—and accepting—that it is neither material progress nor pursuit of knowledge. He advocates turning our attention to our interdependency and learning how to support each other, and our world, with humility, love, and compassion.

Here is where we will discover our true value, not just our personal or commodity or economic value, but rather the universal value that we share with each other. Living according to our universal value, we will regain utopia.

A monk once asked Zen Master Yun-men,
"What is the essence of the supreme teaching?"
Yun-men said, "When spring comes, the grass grows by itself."

—FROM THE GOLDEN AGE OF CHINESE ZEN

Appendix One
Zen Practice

This appendix offers a short orientation to Zen practice, emphasizing the elements most relevant to modern life.

Zazen

The heart of Zen practice is the motivation to sit in meditation (Japanese: *zazen*) on a consistent basis and make one's best effort to maintain awareness. Practicing zazen upon awakening, in the dim morning light, before the first cup of coffee, before engaging in the busyness of life, brings a sense of fulfillment as the light of a new day arises. When the responsibilities of family or work do not allow for early-morning zazen, sitting in the evening or at another time during the day is perfectly fine. When possible, sitting with others in a space dedicated to meditation brings a sense of connection, but if such a place is not readily available, sitting alone is encouraged.

Letting Go

Despite our best efforts, the mind cannot entirely put an end to mental or emotional distractions through willpower. Thoughts, memories, and insights will arise continuously during meditation. The emphasis of zazen is not to stop the mind's activity, but to bring our attention back to the present whenever we recognize that we've become distracted. The point is not to be concerned about distractions, but to gently let go of exciting, disturbing, and entertaining memories, fantasies, and conjectures that arise spontaneously and return to paying attention to one's breath.

Attentive Intimacy

As the mind increases its capacity to return to the present during zazen, it is also improving its skill at being attentive during activities of daily life—at work, at home, on the freeway, or in the market. We become more intimate, less distant, with things and each other. Problems are solved more readily, with less anxiety, while relationships go more smoothly.

Emotions

In addition to memories of the past and imaginings of the future, negative emotions will likely arise to consciousness during zazen. When we begin our practice, we might feel that the meditation itself is producing this discomfort, not realizing that these feelings have been dimly present all along. As the mind softens its instinct to defend itself, these elements are able to come into consciousness more easily, offering us the opportunity to learn how to respond to them in a creative way, rather than being overwhelmed. Over time, as the mind better understands and accepts itself as it is, the arising of these feelings is less jarring and their frequency and sharpness diminishes.

Relationship to Therapy

Meditation practice can be therapeutic, yet Zen practice itself is not therapy, even though both are about relieving suffering by uncovering and honestly facing the activity of the mind. Zen practice does not analyze emotional difficulties nor try to investigate their sources. Rather, it encourages recognition and acceptance of whatever feeling may arise and letting it go by returning attention to the present. In effect, the mind gives itself permission to have a negative feeling by acknowledging, "This is just something happening in this moment." The emotional grip is loosened, leading to relief of anxiety. This doesn't mean that Zen discourages therapy, especially in troublesome situations where deep, unremitting suffering—impacting an individual's capacity to function and find meaning in life—does call for identification and exploration of its sources.

No Striving

The Soto School of Zen Buddhism, founded by Dogen in thirteenth-century Japan and brought to America by Shunryu Suzuki in the twentieth century, discourages engaging in zazen for the purpose of gaining enlightenment—a vision, a flash of wisdom that reveals all truth in an instant, putting a final end to all personal problems. Such a pursuit is seen as contrary to the individual's best interest, as striving to attain something for oneself, even spiritual fulfillment, is just one more desire, adding to suffering. More to the point, enlightenment is already inherent in each of us, not something outside of our ordinary self that needs to be pursued and achieved. Rather, it is to be expressed, or realized, by zazen practice. This is the foundation of Dogen's understanding of Buddhism.

Expressing True Nature

Zazen's quiet activity expresses one's true self, allowing us to experience that we are infinitely more than short-lived creatures of flesh, senses, and emotions hungering for gratification. The unfolding understanding of the reality of worldly phenomena—the reality that exists beyond appearances—releases a confidence unhindered by human frailty and mortality. This confidence is deeper than can be attained in worldly affairs, wider than admiration or reputation. Those things can fade, while confidence based on knowing our true selves cannot be lost. As practice matures, the mind learns to recognize the world as a cohesive, timeless whole, rather than a series of isolated activities and experiences driven by desires and expectations.

Rituals of Work and Ceremony

Over time, Zen students see ordinary activities in a new way, not just as chores but as quiet rituals, the expression of the universal through the particular. Work, usually envisioned as tedious and necessary, is embraced rather than shunned. Zen monasteries emphasize careful attention to simple tasks, like sweeping the floor, cleaning the toilets, cooking, and washing dishes.

Rituals and ceremonies play an important role in the formal practice of Zen. They are not a form of worship toward an external deity or a way to earn merit. Chanting, bowing, and mindful meals taken together in a reverential, carefully orchestrated manner are considered an active extension of sitting practice, continuing the attitude of no-self. As one scholar points out, "As one engages in ritual, one's consciousness changes.... Rituals work through the senses to cultivate wisdom in the bones.... Rituals can help one feel the sense of connectedness bodily."[24]

Taking Care

Zen practice brings together self-discipline and determination with generosity, patience, and a caring attitude toward others. Zazen, work, and ceremonies are expressions of the true nature inherent in all things. Pursued mindfully, they diminish emphasis on personal issues, encouraging in its place selflessness and concern for the well-being of others. These activities enhance the individual's focus, discipline, and "taking-care" attitude. This reverence—expressing inherent enlightenment by being mindful to whatever we are doing in this moment—becomes the basis for well-being.

The importance of taking care of ordinary activities is illustrated by the following story. Two monks are on pilgrimage, traveling from temple to temple, visiting and studying with well-known teachers to expand their practice and understanding. Walking beside a creek, they approach a well-known monastery. A vegetable leaf appears, floating downstream. The monks pause in dismay, and prepare to turn around and retrace their steps. Suddenly another monk comes out of a side door, running toward the creek with a long pole. He stops at the edge of the water, reaching out to retrieve the truant leaf. The two monks smile and quickly resume their journey to the temple.

No Dogma

Zen students are not discouraged from reading philosophical or religious texts, engaging in other faiths, or attending the church, temple, or synagogue of their choice. However, strict adherence to a philosophical belief system is not part of the practice. Suzuki-roshi put it this way:

> I discovered that it is necessary, absolutely necessary, to believe in nothing. That is, we have to believe in something which has no form or color—something which exists before all forms and colors appear. This is a very important point. No matter what god or doctrine you believe in, if you become attached to it, your belief will be based more or less on a self-centered idea.[25]

Subtlety

Zen emphasizes understanding the true nature of all conditioned phenomena, including ourselves. We usually begin by studying transiency, impermanence, and no-self, and the insights into how the mind creates desire and suffering. Reflecting on these ideas helps us appreciate things from a new perspective, not simply according to appearances or "common sense." Ideas, however, are not enough to bring about deep understanding. Awakening takes place only when we allow inherent, subtle wisdom to express itself.

Stilling the mind creates a field in which composure and wisdom can arise. This allows the busy mind to feel its basic quality, beneath the noisiness of everyday life. This is the subtle way of seeing the world, including oneself and others. Without this subtlety, worldly things seem to be "attractive" or "unattractive," an arbitrary mental distinction that engenders either desire or repulsion. Known in Buddhism as duality, it is a primary source of confusion and anxiety. Stillness, on the other hand, yields insight into a world beyond categorizations, perhaps less exciting, but revealing and joyous.

Zen Teachers

Starting with the Buddha and his followers, the teacher and the community have remained vital features of Buddhism. In Zen, the teacher is seen as the one who holds the practice, who brings it forward to the present day, maintaining the connection with the tradition back to Buddha himself. The teacher leads and encourages others, not relying on preaching or admonition, but by setting an example. He or she is always in the meditation hall (zendo) for scheduled zazen. Through the wisdom of his or her study and experience, he or she provides guidance in the practice, giving lectures, personal interviews, and social engagement. With optimism and a supportive attitude, the teacher models ethical behavior and caring, the essential hallmarks of Buddhism.

Most Zen teachers in the United States have had some years of monastic training. However, in contrast to Asia, a good number, perhaps half, have worked or continue to work in the everyday world and lead a more-or-less secular life. These experiences bring real-world relevance to the practice, enabling them to respond to the frequently asked question, "How do I bring my spiritual practice into my everyday life?"

Sangha Community

As in Buddha's original community (Pali: *Sangha*), Zen practitioners bring encouragement and support to each other by practicing together, whether in zazen, work, ceremony, social activities, or administrative business. By nurturing trust and friendship, the Buddhist community provides a sanctuary for its members. Sangha is perhaps the most important element in the Buddhist and Zen worldview, as it represents the universal connection of all things—their inherent, shared oneness.

The Meaning of Forms in Zen Practice
Contributed by Phuong Ertley

Phuong Ertley is a marriage and family therapist in private practice in Palo Alto and San Francisco, a university instructor, and a yoga teacher. She was ordained as a Zen monk in 2016.

When a visitor comes to the meditation hall, he or she notices behaviors that are not customary to contemporary Western society: bowing, silence, folded hands, and an orderly way of moving. This can seem rigid or off-putting to some people. For others, it may be a source of comfort.

Each of the forms has a functional as well as a poetic purpose. Consider silence in the meditation hall. The cumulative lack of talking of eighty or so people creates a cushion of emotional rest. This collective silencing of extraneous thought and pleasantries among people allows for a deeper relationship to grow. The silence, born of the discipline of each person, contributes deeper connections. When you are silent, your thoughts slow down. Your eyes become more alert. Your body becomes more responsive. As you move in silence with others, you begin to notice a flow or order that you can drop into, like swimming in a stream. When you aren't sure how to proceed, the best thing to do is to simply observe what others are doing.

Second, bowing. We bow to Buddha, we bow to the cushion, we bow to the group. What does it all mean? The answer may be unique to each person as she or he practices. In my experience, when I tip my head over, it bends my spine. This bending over invites a feeling of reverence: I'm humbling myself before something. If it's the statue of the Buddha, it reminds me of all I don't know. Life operates on a bigger scale than my small mind. I find it comforting that there is something more than my personal desires and wishes. There's a universal order that is beyond my ken. Our habitual mind always tries to control the events in our lives, especially the ones we deem important. However, I believe we become anxious because we know that we're prone to make mistakes. What a relief it can be to surrender to the fact that we're not responsible for *everything*, and it will all still go well.

When I bow to my *zafu* or meditation cushion, I'm reminded that I'm not alone on this path. The cushion supports me to sit comfortably. If it weren't there, my experience would be more painful. The cushion, situated on its base *zabuton* before my arrival, has also supported countless meditators before me and will continue to support others after me. The cushion reminds me of the other sincere practitioners. Just knowing that others are interested in this path encourages me.

When we sit, we do so with an upright spine, hands folded in our laps, signaling an alert mind. The folded hands are soft, not tense, and self-contained. This gesture reminds me that all that I need is contained in this moment. Everything I need for my spiritual awakening is right here. The point is to be awake and calm, no matter how internally distracted I feel or how loudly others swallow, fidget, or cough. Seat firmly planted and spine tall arouses a confident attitude that says all will be well.

After the sitting practice, we fluff our cushions, wipe off any dust, and ready it for the next person. This action says that I care about who comes after me. I think not only of myself and my needs, but also about others. When I turn toward the center of the room, once again I bow, this time to the community. By bowing, I offer my gratitude for the existence of the Sangha, a group of people who want the same things I do. We're all here to learn a way to live that results in peace and harmony. We take time out of our busy lives to quiet the storms inside, so we may have the clarity to behave respectfully, gratefully, and conscientiously toward others.

To behave well means to behave with discipline. Restraint in speech, restraint in movement, and the ability to detach from thoughts are all forms of discipline. Many of the mistakes we make in life have to do with the lack of consideration for others—a misplaced word, thought, or deed. We've all had experiences with the proverbial foot in the mouth. How many times have we said something that was hurtful, unkind, and not exactly true? Conscientious speech is a daily challenge in our practice.

This is where the ritual of chanting helps us. Chanting in Zen practice involves 90 percent listening and 10 percent vocalizing. In order to chant in harmony with others, we need to listen to the cadence, pitch, and tone of the people around us. It doesn't mean to mimic others, but to participate in a way that it supports the whole group. Be vigorous, yet supportive. Chanting requires a concentrated and pliable mind. Go with the flow and stop when it stops. Don't stand above others, don't drown others out, but also be heard.

Zen practice asks that you participate in all the ways possible: in your actions, your words, your thoughts, and of course, with your heart. It's said that of the three treasures, the Buddha, the Dharma, and the Sangha, the Sangha is the most important. By engaging our minds and bodies in these simple acts, we create a healthy Sangha. By being quiet, alert, and attentive toward ourselves and others, we create an experience of depth and presence for all. Who is the Sangha? It's you and me. By meditating together on a regular basis, we provide for and protect each other's right to an internal life. Spending the time to sit and observe ourselves is much easier with others and quite difficult by ourselves. By doing it together, we create the opportunity and likelihood that we may all grow wise together.

A History of Kannon Do: A Zen Meditation Center in Silicon Valley

Kannon Do brings the spiritual practice of Soto Zen Buddhism to the San Francisco Peninsula and the South Bay, including Mountain View, Sunnyvale, Palo Alto, San Jose, and surrounding communities. Its purpose is to encourage and support a spiritual worldview in lives faced with constant distractions, work and family pressures, and demanding deadlines. Primary activities include meditation, exploring Buddhist teachings, and discovering ways Zen can be expressed in daily life. Kannon Do is a nonresidential center, voluntarily maintained and supported by its members. There are no membership requirements to participate in its activities. The center welcomes all individuals interested in exploring Zen practice.

Zen Master Shunryu Suzuki arrived in the United States in 1959 to be resident priest of Sokoji, the Soto Zen temple in San Francisco's Japantown. He sat alone in meditation (zazen), the congregation deferring to what they felt was a monk's practice. Little by little, though, young people of a new generation discovered Suzuki-roshi and joined him for zazen. In 1961, he and his Zen students founded the San Francisco Zen Center, sharing the Sokoji building with the Japanese American congregation. By the late 1960s, the Zen Center group had grown large enough to need a separate place, and in 1969, the group moved to a beautiful building at Page and Laguna Streets, a mile from Japantown. Suzuki-roshi's life and the early history of Zen Center are well documented in *Crooked Cucumber: The Life and Zen Teaching of Shunryu Suzuki* by David Chadwick.

In 1964, Roshi was visiting Redwood City, south of San Francisco, and remarked that if a good meeting place could be found on the Peninsula, he would like to begin a weekly meditation group. The first gathering was held in the living room of a Stanford graduate student in Palo Alto. Three or four people attended the first few Thursday morning meetings. In April 1965, an evening group was established in Redwood City.

Not long after, the morning group moved to the home of Marian Derby in Los Altos. An informal breakfast followed zazen and Suzuki-roshi's brief lecture. The family-like discussions at the breakfast table with Roshi were as popular as his talks. In 1965, the evening group also moved to Marian's. Tea and cookies were served following the weekly lectures, which sometimes lasted until 11:00 p.m. When Marian's son left for medical school, his room became available for Suzuki-roshi to stay overnight, and so the schedule was changed to Wednesday evenings and Thursday mornings. Most often it was Marian who drove to San Francisco to pick up Roshi and take him home the next day.

Marian began recording Roshi's morning lectures on a huge reel-to-reel Wollensak tape recorder. These "little talks" were rarely longer than fifteen minutes. Marian transcribed the tapes, going over each transcript with Suzuki-roshi. The idea of creating a book from the lectures arose, and it was given the title *Morning Talks in Los Altos*. In 1967, the transcripts were given to San Francisco Zen Center for further editing, and the book was given a new title, *Zen Mind, Beginner's Mind*. In 1968, Trudy Dixon, very ill with cancer at the time, took on the editing. Trudy's deep understanding of Zen and her great gifts as a writer resulted in the respected and influential book, published in 1971 and still an important and widely read introduction to Zen. Trudy passed away before its publication.

After a year of meeting in Marian's living room, the number

of people attending zazen and lectures had grown, and Marian's garage was converted into a meditation hall. Suzuki-roshi designed the traditional Japanese-style zendo, and construction, performed entirely by Sangha members, began in June 1966. Haiku Zendo, named for its seventeen seats that matched the number of syllables in a haiku poem, officially opened on August 4, 1966.

In 1968, Marian went to Tassajara Zen Mountain Center to deepen her practice. Les and Mary Kaye, who had been attending Haiku Zendo gatherings for two years, agreed to move into Marian's home. In 1969, Suzuki-roshi suggested that the Haiku Zendo community invite Kobun Chino-sensei to return to the United States to become resident teacher. He arrived in February 1970 and lived with the Kaye family for nine months. He married Harriet, and they rented a house a block from Haiku Zendo. In January 1971, Les was ordained as a Zen priest by Suzuki-roshi in a ceremony at Haiku Zendo. Roshi passed away from cancer in December of that year.

With Kobun as its spiritual leader, the Haiku Zendo established a steady practice, attracting many from the Peninsula. In 1979, based on the need to create a more accessible and spacious center, the Sangha purchased a small church in a quiet Mountain View neighborhood and named the new zendo Kannon Do, "place of compassion." In 1983, Kobun moved to New Mexico to help establish a new Zen center there, and appointed Les Kaye to be the spiritual leader of Kannon Do. In 1985, Les received dharma transmission, approval to teach and ordain students, from Hoitsu Suzuki, the son and dharma heir of Shunryu Suzuki-roshi, in a month-long ceremony in Japan. In 1988, the Kannon Do Sangha held a Mountain Seat Ceremony installing Les Kaye as its first abbot.

In 1990, the members of Kannon Do decided to grow the center to accommodate its widening activities. Following a decade of fundraising, three years finding a property, a year and a half obtaining permits, and a year of construction, the Sangha moved into the new Kannon Do in Mountain View in 2006. By 2017, membership had grown to nearly 400 members and had spawned new Zen centers in California, Oregon, Maine, France, and Italy. For more about Kannon Do, visit https://kannondo.org.

Notes

1   E. F. Schumacher, *Small is Beautiful: Economics as if People Mattered* (New York: Harper Perennial, 2010), 39.

2   Walpola Rahula, *What the Buddha Taught* (New York: Grove Press, 1959), xv.

3   Karen Armstrong, *Buddha* (New York: Penguin Books, 2001), 1.

4   Kazuaki Tanahashi, ed., *Moon in a Dewdrop: Writings of Zen Master Dogen* (San Francisco: North Point Press, 1985), 72.

5   George Eliot, *Middlemarch* (London: Penguin Books, 1994), 838.

6   See Rick Fields, *How the Swans Came to the Lake: A Narrative History of Buddhism in America* (Boston: Shambhala, 1981).

7   Ibid.

8   Attributed to Tozan Ryokai (807–869 CE), founder of the school of Soto Zen in China.

9   Kadambari Kaul, *Verses from the Dhammapada* (New Delhi: Indialog Publications, 2007), 90.

10 Eihei Dogen, *Shōbōgenzō: Volume I: Sound of the Valley, Color of the Mountain* (Sendai, Japan: Daihokkaikaku Publishing Company, 1975), 91.

11 Ibid., 92.

12   Shunryu Suzuki, *Zen Mind, Beginner's Mind* (New York: Weatherhill, 1970), 40.

13   Tanahashi, *Moon in a Dewdrop*, 97.

14   Ibid., 70.

15   Ibid., 164.

16   David Brooks, *The Road to Character* (New York: Random House, 2015), xii.

17   Ibid., xvi.

18   Ibid.

19   David Chadwick, *Crooked Cucumber: The Life and Teachings of Shunryu Suzuki* (New York: Broadway Books, 1999), 35.

20   Tanahashi, *Moon in a Dewdrop*, 70.

21   Suzuki, *Zen Mind, Beginner's Mind*, 114.

22   1 Corinthians 13:11.

23   Shunryu Suzuki, untitled talk (lecture, San Francisco Zen Center: San Francisco, CA, August 28, 1965).

24   Paula Arai, *Bringing Zen Home: The Healing Heart of Japanese Women's Rituals* (Honolulu: University of Hawaii Press, 2011), 40.

25   Suzuki, *Zen Mind, Beginner's Mind*, 112.

Acknowledgments

I was intrigued when Zen student and international journalist Teresa Bouza suggested that we write a book together presenting the perspectives of men and women in Silicon Valley who combine demanding work and family responsibilities with a daily Zen practice. Now, after twenty-two months of interviewing, writing, and editing, we present this book to you. I'm grateful to Teresa for her vision, her diligence, and her creativity.

Thanks to Jill Wolfson, author, editor, friend, writing coach, and long-time Zen student, whose caring insights gave cohesion and focus to our unruly first draft.

I am indebted to our agent, Arnie Kotler, master craftsman of language, for his creativity, enthusiasm, and guidance.

Many thanks to our editor, Jacob Surpin, and members of the team at Parallax Press, for their imagination and creativity. It was a pleasure to work with such an enthusiastic group.

Teresa and I are grateful to Paul Slakey, Bonnie Sarmiento, Andy Narayanan, Brenda Golianu, Travis Marsot, Scott Williams, Dan Geiger, Victor Legge, Dave Redell, Colleen King Ney, Randy Komisar, Ken Simpson, Jayashree Mahajan, and Jean-Louis Gassée for their willingness to share their stories.

Finally, to my wife Mary, for her infinite patience, unending good humor, no-frills common sense, and quiet wisdom.

About the Authors

Les Kaye has been integrally involved in developing Zen practice in America for over fifty years. He started work in 1958 for IBM in San Jose, California, and for over thirty years held positions in engineering, sales, and management. Les became interested in Zen in the mid-1960s and started Zen practice in 1966 with a small group in the garage of a private home. In 1970, he took a leave of absence to attend a three-month practice period at Tassajara Zen Monastery in California. The following year he was ordained a Zen monk by Zen Master Shunryu Suzuki, author of *Zen Mind, Beginners Mind*. In 1973, he took an additional leave of absence to attend a second practice period, this time as head monk. In 1974, Les received Dharma Transmission, authority to teach, from Hoitsu Suzuki, son and successor to Shunryu Suzuki. In 1985, he was appointed teacher at Kannon Do Zen Center in Mountain View, California. He and his wife Mary have two adult children and live in Los Altos. His first book, *Zen at Work*, includes stories of how his own meditation practice enhanced the quality of his life and work. He is also the author of *Joyously through the Days: Living the Journey of Spiritual Practice*.

Teresa Bouza is an international journalist with extensive experience in Europe and the United States, most recently covering technology and innovation in Silicon Valley. She has worked for *The Wall Street Journal* as well as Spain's global news agency EFE and the Spanish business daily *Cinco Dias*. She is the founder of

Datafest, a computing contest to develop technological solutions to challenges like international migration and life in modern cities. She has led several international and collaborative events. She has worked with engineers, developers, and data experts across the globe, both at universities and in various industries, while organizing the hackathons. Bouza has a master's degree from Columbia University and was a Knight Fellow at Stanford in 2012. Teresa became interested in Zen after a friend told her about *Zen Mind, Beginners Mind* in 2002. She has attended several retreats at Green Gulch Farm Zen Center over the years and started formal practice at Kannon Do in 2015.

Related Titles

Biography of Silence, Pablo d'Ors

The Nest in the Stream, Michael Kearney

No Mud, No Lotus, Thich Nhat Hanh

The Other Shore, Thich Nhat Hanh

The Seven Laws of Enough, Gina LaRoche and Jennifer Cohen

Work That Matters, Maia Duerr

Work, Thich Nhat Hanh

PARALLAX PRESS

Parallax Press, a nonprofit publisher founded by Zen Master Thich Nhat Hanh, publishes books and media on the art of mindful living and Engaged Buddhism. We are committed to offering teachings that help transform suffering and injustice. Our aspiration is to contribute to collective insight and awakening, bringing about a more joyful, healthy, and compassionate society.

For a copy of the catalog, please contact:

Parallax Press
P.O. Box 7355
Berkeley, CA
94707

parallax.org

31901064595467